USABLE TRUTHS

"Irving Feldman writes with an immediacy, vigor, and precision of insight that make this book an exhilarating achievement. Again and again, one is brought to consider the claim of unwelcome doubts as well as unsolicited truths. His discipline and economy of phrase can survive comparison with the masters of the aphorism." —David Bromwich, Sterling Professor of English at Yale University

"Aphorisms, shrewd observations, rules to live by and rules to resist—such are Irving Feldman's usable truths. Some produce short, sharp shocks of recognition; others need to be lingered over and lived with, unpacked like a line of metaphysical poetry. In each the fewest words enfold the fullest meaning. Like aphorists before him, Feldman looks at love and age and the way we live now, but he brings a poet's touch to even his most philosophical insights. *Usable Truths* is thus what the French call a perfect *livre de chevet*, a book to keep on a bedside nightstand, ideal for those moments before sleep when we reflect on the strange turnings, the hits and misses, in our own lives." — Michael Dirda, Pulitzer Prize-winning critic for *The Washington Post* and the author of several collections of essays, most recently *Browsings: A Year of Reading, Collecting, and Living with Books.*

"'Usable' because these aphorisms invite us to trace—with mordant wit but also pity, and a strange courtesy—the secret life of our loves, hatreds, wonders, lies, and vanities, our forms of praise and styles of doubt, to trace their secret gifts and secret wounds, wherein we and others around us may gain and lose more than we think. They ask you to work on your creaturely listening. —Kenneth Gross, Alan F. Hilfiker Distinguished Professor of English, University of Rochester

"*Usable Truths* is an aphoristic treasure chest. It invites the reader to reach in up to the elbows, certain to retrieve marvels of insight, satire, deflation of our vanities, celebration of our generosities, wordplay for the play's sake, sentences built to please, provoke, press us into self-knowledge." —Alicia Ostriker, Author of *Waiting for the Light*, New York State Poet Laureate

"In *Usable Truths*, Irving Feldman joins Pascal, La Rochefoucauld, Blake, Emerson and a handful of other epigrammatists who alert us, with their laconic wit and wisdom, to the mansions that the mind can build in and from the smallest rooms of incisive thought. These nuggets contain a trove of riches." —Willard Spiegelman, Hughes Professor of English, Emeritus, at Southern Methodist University

PRAISE FOR

IRVING FELDMAN'S POEMS

"It is an enormous pleasure to read through Irving Feldman's *Collected Poems*. The spirit of the mordantly exuberant Moshe Leib Halpern, best of all Yiddish poets, lives again in Feldman's work: a poignant comedy that is also the true history of both an intense life and a tragic era."— Harold Bloom

"*Collected Poems* is more than a book. It's a cornucopia. Out of it spill the most amazing poems, one after another telling us who we are—with joy in the telling, even when the truths told are painful. Feldman's is the joy of recreating with such virtuosity the world of his experience, which is also our world, the world of all of us here; it is the joy of invoking and fashioning our American language and itys astonishing life to give us so much pleasure." — David Ferry

"Moving from stretches of savage indignation … to moments of plangent lyric, Feldman's high and passionate diction often comes as close to nobility as one might dare to suggest … Feldman is one of our very best poets, and he is certainly unique today in his access to a prophetic force." — John Hollander

"Irving Feldman's voice in this half-century collection is a choir of multiplicity, ranging from the cosmically Miltonic to the up-to-minute vernacular: he is a psalmist and satirist, elegist and stand-up comic, mandarin and graffiti artist, philosopher and town-crier, romantic and skeptic. His heartbreaking 'Pripet Marshes' will stand, in its intimate and afflicted grandeur, with Auden's 'September 1, 1939' as one of the great poems of the twentieth century." — Cynthia Ozick

"If one measure of poetic greatness is the ability to redefine the limits of what poetry can do, *The Life and Letters* is a great book, astonishing in its range of language and invention, and utterly enthralling in its combination of irreverent humor, linguistic play, and deadly insight. Feldman's sensibility combines and integrates in remarkable ways intellectual suspiciousness and lyric, almost visionary, reach. … He is America's postmodern Alexander Pope. He is outrageously funny, profoundly wise, and wholly free of the fashions, pieties and pretensions that limit the work of most of his contemporaries." — Alan Shapiro

"[Feldman is] one of the most engaging and powerful poets of his generation." — Lionel Trilling

USABLE TRUTHS

USABLE TRUTHS

APHORISMS & OBSERVATIONS

IRVING FELDMAN

WAYWISER

First published in 2019 by

THE WAYWISER PRESS

Christmas Cottage, Church Enstone, Chipping Norton, Oxfordshire, OX7 4NN, UK
P. O. Box 6205, Baltimore, MD 21206, USA
https://waywiser-press.com

EDITOR-IN-CHIEF
Philip Hoy

SENIOR AMERICAN EDITOR
Joseph Harrison

ASSOCIATE EDITORS
Eric McHenry | Dora Malech | V. Penelope Pelizzon | Clive Watkins | Greg Williamson | Matthew Yorke

ISBN: 978-1-904130-99-4

2 4 6 8 10 9 7 5 3 1

Printed and bound by
T. J. International Ltd., Padstow, Cornwall, PL28 8R

To

RICHARD HOWARD

Brother in Art

Old Friend

ALSO BY IRVING FELDMAN

*　*　*

Courtesy came before joy.
The greeting preceded the recognition.

To be responded to is as close as one comes in this life to immortality.

The work that sustains itself surpasses itself.

The prisoner of dialectics can never cease rattling his chain.

The fullness of possibility is not abolished by any actuality.

The language isn't saved by style but by a tale worth telling.

How much complexity is brushed aside by a courteous greeting.

No atheists in foxholes? No theologians, either.

Every time a truth is told the world is larger.

Asceticism is properly directed not toward diminishing desire but toward preventing satiety, thereby preserving desire.

What is at work in fun is purity of heart.

It is good to feel my feelings, exquisite to feel yours.

At every instant, we will one another alive, and should one die, it is, beyond loss, our defeat.

Our least gift to our heirs wills them an entire world willing them here.

No state can be governed without law and order and graft.

A taste for satire gives one, particularly in youth, the illusion of having a personality.

Of her cancer the dying courtesan contrives a charm.

We boast to triumph over our hypersensitivity by rendering it insensitive.

Telling makes what was accidental and alien deliberate and therefore one's own.

Seductive, she wants most of all to feel herself seducing, feel herself slowly succumbing to her powers of seduction. And how great they must be when she who knows herself so well succumbs to herself!

The voluble man is as vain of his reasons as he is shameful of his acts.

Great enterprises entail great risk. She believes in God, Nature, and cosmetics.

Paperwork, unlike the crafts, has no scale.

Unable to give themselves, they demand submission. They desire power where surrender failed.

His laconicism is his defense against his drive toward silence.

The experts wish to forbid us anything so amateurish as a life.

Art operates as a refining mystery.

The artist who believes he need please no one but himself will succeed beyond his wildest dream.

The kitchen mystery: here death becomes food.

Is all the religious wisdom in the world meant only to enable shopkeepers to get up and go down and open their shops in the morning?

When the lion dies, rabbits roar.

The indestructibility of the lost world is the fundamental subject of faith.

"Benevolent despot." A child's dream, if only to show his parents the kind of despotism they should practice toward him.

Tragedy consoles by revealing the original.

To seduce with the truth is not more moral than to seduce with lies.

Lacking the power of action, we discover our power of opinion – heart's affirmation or heart's veto. Wondrous revelation this power so long unused, so easy to use, so transforming. Of everything there is we can say, "I like it." "I don't like it."

Man is the animal who imagines itself man.

Flatter a woman and she is grateful for the attention. Flatter a man and he believes it.

Parsimony is a poor critical principle. Richer works can afford to say more than they need to say.

The facets, the conception, do the work: they focus the light. What remains is to be clear.

Addendum to La Rochefoucauld. The man who boasts he can't be flattered has yet to find the right flatterer. *Au contraire, cher maître,* he *has* – himself.

Don't think because you're on the side of the angels the angels are on your side. The angel at your elbow is, however grand and glowing, just you all over again.

A witty king is a weak king.

Mighty epics do not from little insights grow.

A decade dead, and their luster gone after them into the dark: poets who were immortals so long as they were news.

After Kafka. A snow leopard breaks into the temple and drinks from the sacred chalices. He does this night after night. Soon everyone believes himself a snow leopard. Thus was born the Church of the Holy Subversion.

The knight may overlook no evil as too trivial, or poor in pedigree – or his sword will fail when the "worthwhile" evil arrives.

No people celebrates its success in colonizing the land of the dead.

Each vitality creates its immortality, however briefly.

Nixon was a devil put on Earth to tempt man to self-righteousness.

No greater rage than that of the son of a disgraced father, who has denied him his heritage of manhood while polluting it with death.

Art is solving problems – then finding better problems, better solutions.

The mark of the academic is the presence of ideas in the absence of thought.

Youthful conceit gives way in time to mature selfishness.

It is a very small step from manipulating oneself to please others to manipulating others to please oneself.

In art, as in life, shock and speed inhibit feeling.

Pleasure and pessimism go together (as do action and optimism), because pleasure foresees its cessation.

Translation is the parasite its host devours.

Big man. Little woman. Here's the truck. Here's the truck driver.

"Don't call me, I'll call you," says the vulture who will be sure to ring when you no longer answer.

The successful find in flattery the intimacy success has cost them, and makes them crave.

She: And now you'll never be able to hurt me again.
He: How can you say such a thing to me!

How nice if the bad money that drives the good money out were always *very* bad money.

What we do: create, assert, assess, debate, acknowledge value.

The signal human activity is creating value. This the compromised, the corrupt, the humiliated, inauthentic, accursed spirit cannot do – and the innocent does.

Poems are creatures we put into the world to respond to us, and to whom we, in turn, respond. And marvelously there's always room for more.

Ideologues are sentimentalists. They love the names of things.

The realm of error is infinite; the ingenuities of folly are creative beyond prediction.

It is a question whether one prays in order to act well or acts well to better pray.

The rich don't feel called on to render accounts. The world's demands never reach them entrenched behind their bulwark of bucks.

Pomposity is often endearing because we see in it a child puffed up to play an adult, though not so well as we do.

Fine to play devil's advocate, but do be certain it's not a stupid devil.

Unlike horizontal and vertical, depth is conjectural – and therefore the dimension of anxiety.

Clarity is transparency made visible.

Every renunciation renounces a distraction, gains an increment of concentration.

Our parents spring fully grown from our brows.

Poetry is not a craft, but poets are craftsmen. They possess the craft-attitude: detached, they want to make it good – but what this "it" is and how to get to it they can learn only through trial and error.

"Sentimentality" adds self-love to sentiment.

She was telling the novel of their love, while he sat beside her like a pair of bookends.

There is also a violent and abusive flattery.

Time cannot make more stale or repetition perfect its dullness: the true cliché is born, not made.

One is never too old to be a child and receive a blessing, or too young to give one.

Astrology. Every birth makes the stars come true.

Warning! This mind is posted. Raise your head in the jungle of his attention and you will be shot dead.

The strong can bear it, but the weak find bullshit encumbers.

The confident, whatever their uncertainties, can never understand the painful estrangement of those who lack confidence altogether.

Lyric words come to us as being listened to, as having been listened to – in the first place by the poet who set them down. We listen to the words, and we join their society of listeners.

The weakest hands seize the heaviest ax.

There, on the city streets, even prey grows bold, for fear it won't be taken for predator.

We have the strength of our obstacles: as strong, or weak, as Hercules battling taffy.

We don't find it sufficient to live only in fact: each of us wishes to believe he lives by right – occupying the place his forebears prepared for him.

Pascal has it there would be no evil if men had the strength to remain in their rooms – nor, he neglected to add, any good.

Speed is its own milieu.

Our feeling that justice belongs to an objective order in which our judgments participate. Is there any other objectivity we know so intimately?

However deep its source, passion flows swiftly because it flows in a familiar channel, and carries us along so swiftly we fail to notice the channel.

True, there is much self-love in passion, since passion stirs up everything, surface wave and muddy bottom.

She was fighting for her life, while he was a dilettante of feeling — with the result she appeared to be unscrupulous and he an idealist.

The lover, making the gift of his passion, will not permit his beloved to say, "Oh, I wanted something else."

Why is there something and not nothing?
Because we have been spared.

Each man dreams alone, but dreams with the words of all men.

Why must we die? So stories can be told of us.

What kind of leprosy is not leprosy? Rich man's leprosy.

The child believes parents can be used without being used up.

A poem made with care gives the same pleasure as a healthy and belovèd baby.

Our forgotten poets, whose posterity died with them.

For the artist the rule of reason cedes to the rule of thumb.

Idealist: *"Hypocrite!"*
Hypocrite: *"Hypocrite manqué!"*

If B. is "perfectly clear," then he is lying; he tells the truth only when he fudges.

A light touch requires confidence in one's audience.

In your acts of self-congratulation, look for the lie.

Genocide intends to destroy a people's immortality, its right to exist. Who was not killed in the flesh is murdered in spirit – or, killed in the flesh, is murdered again.

Those in position to evoke our sympathy and fail, earn our antipathy.

A terrible storm at sea. What great ship went down one can't imagine from this old turd washed up on the beach.

Rhythm is habit raised to rapture.

I sacrifice myself here in order to reassemble myself there.

Sex, she feels, takes from her, where affection adds. One lumps her with all women; the other singles her out.

The precocious child grows more astonishing every day. Look, eighty years old and his eyes, how bright they are!

The severance of art from cult has sent the former on its dizzying course of novelty.

Inevitably, Bluebeard's wife grew a little aqua around the gills.

At its most intense, consciousness perceives everything as consciousness.

Novels soften the iron law of manifestation – that we are confirmed only as we manifest ourselves – by showing us and so confirming the unmanifested interiors of their characters.

In the city, each insists he is singular, but all are haunted by the one double: disaster.

Doubles are mysterious because they are finally unknowable; figments, they lack metaphysical status, existing without the right to exist.

Doubles terrify because they make your metaphysical status questionable, before they seize it and leave you the double.

Not the one following you, worry about the one up ahead, whose double you may be.

Unlike enmity, competition requires cooperation. And this absence of a collaborator adds to the pain of hatred. Hatred is a game played alone.

Each loves according to his nature and circumstances. Everyone hates in the same way.

Two is the number of domination and subordination; three is the number of politics.

To name is to confer consciousness. Named now, things are intelligences, gaze back and name us anew.

Our streets are crowded with these Diogenes searching one another's eyes, crying, "Why is no one looking for me?"

Just as there is "puppy love," there is "puppy self-love."

The richness of a work lies in its ability to change along with us, while refusing to let us remain boringly, mortally ourselves.

However she moves, she is caught in the amber mucilage of his gaze whose evenness mesmerizes her. "He is," she says, "serious."

Nihilism is the price we pay for avoiding tragedy.

Social events require sponsors. Some boast they introduced bride and groom; others covet the office of gossip to the divorce.

Had Freud been a businessman his psychology might have seen man not as a miserable congeries of defense mechanisms but as enterprising and engaged with his freedom.

His land, his purpose, his mortality: the indissoluble elements of the father's legacy.

Rooster is no law in the henhouse.

Imitation is the highest form of misquotation.

We are instinctively respectful of the intentions of other creatures.

Idealism stands guard over the entire realm of feeling.

In prose, the possible versions multiply; in verse, cadence constrains to the single unalterable one. Robert Lowell, late, rewrote his poems endlessly, unable to find the cadence.

Scum sinks to the top.

Our love-momentum careens headlong forward in the hope of hitting a wall, something, someone, to relieve us of this unbearable instability. Naturally, we believe this our gift to the wall.

Epiphanies are bits of decayed prophecy, since what most concerns the human animal is knowing the future.

We ask our lesser leaders to serve us, ask our greater to serve an ideal that ethical inspiration may carry us out of ourselves.

The needy rich are always with us.

She came to love and bickered to stay.

To find a bargain is to experience grace.

Something for nothing, windfall, freebie, free booze, especially: firewater in my veins. I celebrate my luck, my luck celebrates me. I feast on tender messages from the Universe, which this very instant loves me madly.

The poets of "spontaneity" hurry away from their poor waifs as if these were not their offspring but their excrement.

Grant me the mercy of making sense.

Such the gravitational force of Being, the liar imagines, in his very act of lying and however vaguely, a world in which his lie is true – not a lie, then, but a fiction.

By the same token, you become – in accommodating his lie –another, a fictive, a weightless, self.

Is it the young above all who desire a lingo in which it is impossible not to be profound?

The oldest technology: one man is beating another.

Consisting of sample questions and sample answers, "interviews" are colloquies between third persons.

"Talent" isn't a winning hand – it's what you ante up to get into the game.

Going away to school meant finding a compass and losing a world.

His making comforts him by bringing the maker to repose in the abidingness of substance – however he may twist and tear to shape it.

Kate, settling for second best: "If you can't be kind, at least be fair."

Desiring to give pleasure, we place ourselves in debt to those who in kindness to us take it.

The con man takes his victim, for all his worldly experience, to a place he's never been, which the sucker – disoriented, giddy now – thrills to inhabit. Call this *Sucker's Beatitude*, for which, despite later disillusionment, the sucker will never cease to be grateful.

The soldier went on killing to avenge himself on the one who stole his innocence: that first one he killed.

To those who lack feelings the world arrives without form or force or point or proportion, a fungible sludge of information. Frightened, cold, clueless, confused, they provoke to elicit a response so overt that, finally, they'll "get it."

The great leader, self-mesmerized, believes his people follow him mesmerized by his greatness. If this were so, they would sacrifice nothing for him. He roars, and they see a waif who mews, and want to nurse the little one and keep him safe – all the while they dream of the great leader who one day will come.

He says his feelings are hurt – but they were unkind feelings before they were hurt feelings.

Jake's ambition is like a drummer boy who bangs the fiddle strings, who makes the flute go *boom!*

You call "evil" what defeats your sympathy, your belief that nothing is wholly unlike you and beyond the power of your sympathy to assimilate, since you are (as your innocence would have it) the measure of all things. Evil wakes you to the world.

Puffing and puffing, last year's wannabes chase after this year's Avant-bandwagon.

Some people are incapable of whispering. Some are incapable of understatement.

Because – defenseless – the figures on the TV screen cannot look back at us and forbid our staring, our gaze grows impertinent, and we harden ourselves to do without response. TV viewing is a school in rudeness.

The irrationalists believe making sense is easy. Maybe so. What isn't so easy is making interesting sense.

Standoffish, he is, in secret, Archimedes pondering the distance needed to lift up, in the first place, you and, after you, the Universe.

Owning nothing and owed nothing, powerless, the young flock to the guru who, renaming this and that to reveal the secret nomenclature of power, imparts his one power to them: the power of words.

The "imperfection" of language – that we have more emotions and their nuances than we have names for – enables literature. What we have are single exceedingly long words for exceedingly complex sets of facts, feelings and relations. One such word is *War and Peace* – which had to be invented before it could enter the lexicon, and has, moreover, the power to alter its meaning each time it is read while at the same time never naming anything else.

The same event that makes the naughty nice makes the nice nicer. But then, mightn't they have been nicer all along? Not so nice of them, you think, not to have been nicer than they needed to be.

Translation substitutes fidelity to the text for the concern that brought the original into being and still, at whatever distance, maintains it there.

Any anthology – any museum – is a forest of screams of works torn from the contexts and circumstances, the lived world of their creation.

Unlike the old palaces, the modern pinacotheca is a mall-museum whose abstract surfaces abolish history for the timelessly contemporary, a nowhere's now. The works on its walls, forever new, know nothing but one another.

Tragic theater turns inward. The drama, enforcing the obsession locking its characters together, sees nothing but itself. Comic theater opens itself to the world with topical references.

You write to have yourself understood immediately, in the twinkling of an eye. No, you write in gratitude you were understood before you wrote. You write, then, in order to make the intelligence that is the world manifest itself – in the twinkling of an eye.

The fundamental questions of criticism are the questions greeting any stranger: Who are you? Where do you come from? What do you want?

The vital illusion created by mimesis is not that the work is or presents a "real" world but that there is another, a real, world outside and parallel to that of the work – in which the work's fiction is "real," has consequences, is concernful. In this, the playful art-world and doomed real world are simultaneously present.

"Happiness" is less a state of feeling or being than a category of understanding.

The mana of celebrity: its power to turn strangers into accomplices in your happiness.

Art comes from writing into the teeth of obsession. Successful artist is failed bore. Successful bore is failed artist.

Our range of sympathy is limited by the disgusting and the ridiculous, these guardians who prevent us – until dotage – from falling back into infancy.

Like rhyme and meter, making sense is an obstacle that forces us to penetrate our material.

The warrior's code permits him to run away without loss of face. He knows the "medicine" he lacks today may be his tomorrow.

Fame magnifies the self by incorporating into it all those who know its name, so one need ever be alone – which is generally taken to be the worst that can befall a person.

One main use of meter is to contribute to formality of utterance by providing secondary stresses, which keep the language from falling into the slurrings and elisions of ordinary speech.

Crudely graven or not graven at all, imbued with the communicant's faith, stick or stone will summon forth the god. Without this faith, the image is severed from the god, no representation brings him forth; the communicant has become a connoisseur of approximations.

He spoke with the voice of a loser at poker, a man who knows the bet he announces is so stupid it is utterly gratuitous.

The artist is seer and maker, but controls only the making; his "vision" is simply what his audience finds concernful – and this no artistic skill can create, though its absence may vex and destroy concernfulness.

Poetic speech and sacred speech are alike formulaic: these words and only these words will summon forth the listening god – or, in the case of the poet's fellow listeners, close the gap endemic to all communication, again and again returning the listener from paraphrase, from hearing his own words, to listen more intently to these and only these words. Whatever speech does this is poetic speech.

Obscurity in the lyric poem is self-limiting: wherever the reader's paraphrase replaces the poem's words the poem has ceased to exist, or exists unstably in a peek-a-boo with its paraphrases.

No bad marriage so bad as marriage to a bad conscience.

Redemption restores its innocence, enables the damaged soul to create value again.

The ability to create value originates in a mother murmuring its name over and over and instilling in her infant its soul, its unique and inexhaustible worth, its ability to create value.

No poverty so poor it has no secrets.

He's desperate, defending Trump's corruption. Look, he says, there's corruption everywhere, hell, *everyone* is corrupt. He's unaware corruption, his own, has spoken here. Nor can he know. Creeping, uncontainable, corruption is a gangrene of consciousness, and of hope that brightens it.

Since the substance of a confession in a "confessional" poem or memoir can't be verified – and is often known to be false – the genre isn't defined by its scandal but by the reader who accords fundamental value to its being, in fact, true, without which the work would have little interest for him. Vulgarizing, this reader prefers the journalism of the doomed self to the paradise of the self imagined.

The moment of charmed equipoise of the perfected pace of lyric lingering: you are content to be where you are while, equally content, you are moving along.

I do not know if I shall merit the prize – but who among us is worthy to bestow it?

Has anyone observed that until the last 100 years or so all fiction was written in the past tense? – which works to ventilate and refresh the past's fatedness of fact (what happened had to happen) with fiction's openness of possibility: this story didn't have to happen, and yet, in imagination, in the telling, it happens every time you hear it. What was and is once and once only has been set free to live forever. The mere present tense is barren.

Past-tense narrative establishes a balance between the story and its reader or hearer, which the present tense collapses in offering a false immediacy of action and not, as the past tense does, the real immediacy of reading, or hearing.

In the past tense all things are simultaneously present; and the death they escape in being summoned into presence is also present. Herein lies the power of the past tense.

Wonder is the womb where value grows.

Readers and listeners, we, present here and now, are the future of the story's pastness – and, therefore, the imagination, the hope and freedom, in which the story lives on beyond itself.

Her "heroic criticism" means to affect the course of poetry. But poets have no interest in paths criticism indicates or forbids, only in the power of a new idiom to take them where it will.

We say to the thaumaturge: Slay me to save me.

"The past is another country" that quickly shades into being another world, where all and everyone are legendary, beings made of words.

Tragedy repeated becomes farce. Farce repeated turns to disgust.

An advance, though spurned, leaves in its wake a keloid furrow.

"Of course, I would lie to you to make you happy."
"What else have you done to make me happy?"

Because she knows that at bottom she can count on no one but herself, she compromises from necessity. Snug in the nook the world's prepared for him, he, in compromising, fulfills himself.

Bush: Being saved was just a better way of not having to grow up.

People complain of not being listened to, while welcoming the freedom of not being heard.

Keeping up with the Joneses means keeping up with the Joneses' illusions, coveting their fridge and also their dream that coveted the fridge, however too intimately awful it would be to *be* the Joneses.

Reflection is skeptical – up to the point it becomes an action launched into the unknown; superstitious now, it rubs talismanic bits of lexicon to bribe or beguile what powers guard the pathways of a thought.

Wish someone in Hell, and you will be on hand to greet him.

The ontological status of a lie is already vexed. And even this is snatched away when it is declared obsolete, a supernumerary in the choir of necessary lies. Pity the poor lie!

After Sam lost a bundle on the market, Sid cashed in his envy, bought some sympathy, and still had lots of dough left over.

Making every different thing yield up its tiny quiddity of sameness, monomania is boring, monomania is inventive, monomania is powerful.

Patience says, "If not this time, then next time – it is all *one* time."

One may be – no, one must be – redeemed a hundred times in a day. And still redemption is not less real for being ephemeral.

Why this fashion for reading aloud far too fast? – as if the death-defying feat of a sword-swallower who, if he breathes, he dies.

– Was Yeats' monkey gland surgery elective?
– Yes, but not for the monkey.

Troubled or in doubt, the human animal seeks to right its world in offering up a sacrifice. Sacrifice is our panacea, even for the illness of being well.

Misanthrope won't tread the turf another misanthrope has marked. Not to share his baleful distinction, he insists he'll have a Hell of his own.

Wind doesn't move through space – wind is space moving.

Small talk's comfort of tiny thoughts pattering about the house.

A person who is self-aware, and conscious, therefore, of being observed: this is the essence of theater – without which not theater but peep show.

Whatever the variety of texts, it's always the same boring old meta-text.

Fascinating vulnerability of the predator isolated inside his hunger – those fearsome teeth, that ferocious ignorance of everything else.

The greatest conspiracy of all operates in plain sight: the conspiracy to make the world safe for mediocrity.

Wit. I can taste it in my mouth. Sweet as candy.

What we now deem "ornament" began as the mark of the maker or owner or dedicatee. Its absence declares the thing no one's, and lures subversive vandal hands to add ornamentations of their own.

Since its pathos suits our managerial time, the Freudian view likely to endure is that of a manager-self, the "ego," defensively negotiating its harrowed, brief tenancy hemmed between landlord Superego and Id's barbarian horde of squatters.

Kindness creates the bounty it bestows. We give what we didn't know we had until we gave it.

Feeding the children, we overcome chaos;
their eating blesses the food, blesses
the monotonous manna of our lives, feeds
our hunger for meanings. It is our commonest
form of prayer, naming the bread-word in the bread.
The blessing, too, they eat; the blessing's blessed;
eternity emerges at its growing point.

I suffer if I say too soon, "Now it's my time to receive." We suffer only in our stinginess.

And the sons of the Bosses shall order around the Workers' sons even unto the seventh generation.

A woman will examine a man for the marks of a mother on him, for where a mother went a woman may follow.

Love's purifying intensity makes love unmemorable. Therefore, women wise in the ways of love mix in impurities, create disappoint-ments, misunderstandings, intermittences – and give love epic am-plitude, heroic vigor, and make it worth the telling.

Imagine the judgment of Galatea "paused in the portal of stone" in transit between two worlds, turning away from us, going home.

Patience isn't a special kind of action, but a basic constituent of all actions, since we can say of everything, "It takes time."

However ancient our residence, we are the latecomers, and rent our lot from those first on this ground: the landlords the gods.

The fundamental imperative:
Don't get left behind – or you will be picked off.

Power corrupts, and – since power is in essence ungovernable, illimitable – thinking power corrodes thought.

Power begins in mystery and remains at every point mysterious – and is most mysterious not in its exercise over others but in anyone's compulsion to submit.

Conspiracy theories are stupidity's intellectual elegance.

Great men ignore the canons of good taste; among the kinds of courage they possess is the courage to be banal.

Only if you take your neighbor as seriously as you take yourself will you have a self to be taken seriously – by your neighbor, by yourself.

"Political correctness" provides a structure of taboos for a society where no speech is otherwise forbidden.

It is comeliness of heart in which she adorns her person.

Lying out in their stone habitat, grimed, abject, bored, exposed to any casual or impertinent stare: the fauna of the urban zoo.

So gentle his nihilism one doesn't realize he is saying, All is appearance, all is illusion, and nothing is but words, words that mean nothing.

The Freudian notion of "over-determination," muddling together causation with interpretation, made possible the Miracle of the Multiplying Viewpoints celebrated daily on a thousand campuses. Since no interpretation can be wrong, everyone gets to stick his spoon in the pudding, and the more you stir the more there is!

A formulaic phrase any substitute for which (no matter how original and especially if original) is immediately suspect: *I love you.*

Life imitates bad art, too.

There is order in the universe in so far as I require myself to make sense.

Praise that children know undeserved leaves them feeling they will never deserve it. Defeated, they are cynical: value itself loses its worth – as do we who praise them.

Like a skater, the reader traces out the elegant figure of a piece of wit and, rejoicing in his nimbleness, feels suddenly free and happy to be alive.

Impossible to woo the truly corrupt.

When you give up your child you become your child. If you are single, you have married yourself.

The inimitable: To do it at all, you have to do it all.

Nagging always works – too late: resisted for oneself, then passed on to others.

Mystery of the hero in whom are united exemplary courage and uncontrollable fury.

Our American style, poor in ceremony, is not to add a grace, not to make an incident an occasion.

"Don't you admire me?" the mousetrap asks the mouse, whose bulging eyes are eloquent. "So, I'll take that for a 'Yes.'"

The Fury is derided by minuter, madder furies.

Memories of pleasures past give current pleasures a quality of goodness, of being the world's pleasure no less than your own.

A light touch requires confidence in one's audience.

A woman tells a man, *Never trust a woman.* What does she know? Is it the creature in a dungeon cell, shorn, stripped of every allure, and doomed to stay unloved and alone – alone but for all those women whispering?

The brutal conceit of these "visionaries" who demand everyone change because they've discovered selflessness.

Lawyer, critic, shrink – the glamor of the kibitzing professions: Always out in the storm. Never get wet.

Lacking its vitality of meaning and value, the image is the effigy of a symbol.

Celebrity is a spiritual fascia enveloping the world, then dipping down to touch this or that one and connect him and her to every other angel of the moment.

Things don't just lie around waiting to be referred to by words. Words and things in their cohabitation are alike changed in their exchanges.

Every girl has a dream, every woman a story.

Modesty will preserve itself if only behind a single thread, behind, even, a single thread divided in two. So, the exhibiting self says of the exhibited self, "He (formerly me)."

They are excited by and indulgently condone "bad boy" men – who make them feel again as free as girls.

For the space trapped in a building another space was opened in the earth.

An impertinent query merits the response: "Would you think it rude of me not to answer your question?"

The point of self-discipline is to make the slave in me unavailable to any master other than myself.

Realism tosses its grit of "little, true facts" into the wind of words to give it force, make it do work, move something – and so save it and us from weightless omnipotence.

"Man is an audacity seeking confirmation." (Buber) This is why the best "therapy" is a pat on the back and a helping hand.

The novelist's rite of passage requires him to betray his family. In the poet's trial, he must leave his sanctum of self-idealization.

Many a marvelous woman has gone to Hell to prove to some fool he underestimates her.

Hermits of space, the wanderers.

Believers wish to be believed. Thinkers try to make sense.

A eulogy spoken by a stranger, a professional eulogist at his third funeral that morning. What he says is hasty, banal, ignorant, repeats the very clichés he put in your mouth to then elicit from you. Hearing them said aloud, you sit there sobbing, saying to yourself, "This is right. This is right."

My heart is full. Only the speech
of the ritual can express it.

Like the dark side of the moon – where all the orphan furniture is stored – nothing in the blind woman's home was meant to be looked at, nothing having been seen.

Any word any thought raised against me or mine slays me, and requires me to arise and reclaim our right to be.

My compass of composition has for its cardinal points: *Too heavy. Too light. Too fast. Too slow.* They tell me where I am off-course.

They blame the "limitations" of language who – from laziness, perhaps – have yet to test the limits of their imaginations.

We are able to distinguish fine gradations of inauthenticity, of illegitimacy in others and in ourselves – and, therefore, the dubious value these produce.

Salesman sells by imposing his will. If buyer submits, he brings home that occupying alien force of will coupled to this familiar, faintly nauseating sense of humiliation.

The master's jest becomes the acolytes' law, a king's whim his people's despair.

Imagination isn't particular inventions but the transposition of the whole into the realm of the possible.

Why has the hug replaced the handshake? Because actors – to show off their lovableness – want the largest, least ambiguous gestures.

In the hug, eyes don't meet, and the handshake's nuances are lost – to be replaced by the rude, solitary expressiveness of each one's eyes behind the other's back.

The right thing to do is also the most elegant.

Without a class system and its established "reality" to contend against, Surrealism in America doesn't subvert, it decorates.

Dullness to the dull is pleasure.

An economy of pennies the poor share with children – and with the child in any rich man.

Old teachers are given to a rusing, obscene charm because, like courtesans, they have tried for too many years to interest students who didn't interest them.

Praise is spiced with danger – to the praised one exposed to the backlash's swipe, to the praiser diverting an offering due a god.

I offer, "We assume – rapturously, wrongly – praise licenses itself. As with any approach to a person, we have first to receive permission to praise." "Sir, license to praise me was stipulated at the world's creation. Proceed immediately to sublime caresses."

Devil confesses not to purge himself. Devil confesses to pollute.

Nostalgia for "creativity" belongs to the spectator; disengaged, idle, doubting the reality before him, he yearns to have his hands in the clay, and say with the creator, "This thing *is*. I made it. I *know*."

Metrical stress, which happens to syllables, is automatic and non-sensical. Rhythm, emphasizing words – in the light of meaning (and much else) – has at every instant to be found and made by the reader, and, therefore, is creative.

Consumption destroys, and consumers are driven by despair to consume more and more, and heap its void with more excrements of void.

Cycled through the black box of the Unconscious, what entered as the symptom emerged as its cause. So you dig up the treasure you buried, and are no richer.

When Randy got Sally to dump him, he was chipper, "Sally dumped me. So, life goes on." So, life went on, with its usual good spirits and bad faith.

Imagine a debate between a sane liar and a madman who tells the truth.

Job's faith rendered God's power moral – until God showed his power's overwhelming self-sufficiency, and taught Job his faith was no more than feeling, and suited only to worshiping power.

Poets, corrupted by their isolation from an audience, don't know when they bore. Where this is cured, new opportunities for corruption arise.

Corrupted audiences don't know when they're bored.

What counts is not how well you burnish the lamp but how it shines.

This insomniac kibitzer has moved into your skull. And he's angry you've given him your lousy hand to play. He smells bad, too. Failure means you're never alone and don't get to pick your friends.

When both give and both receive, neither need envy the other.

Too much irony gave him so strong a sweet tooth for bad tastes these became indistinguishably the taste of himself.

Pain can't be shared and pleasure not shared is suffered.

Success is being wooed by an avalanche.

Keep your own counsel. Never let them know what you're thinking. Be strong, like a stone. Filled with your self-satisfied palaver and understanding only palaver, do you dare gainsay his animal cunning?

At every instant, we test in thought against ourselves the power and swiftness of the course of things – not to be carried away, not left behind.

We are always ready to throw the drowning man a towel.

How often a woman will feel she's robbed her husband of his freedom – for which she lives a constant, numbing, shaming apology. And all the while she suspects he has no idea what freedom is. Had she his freedom, oh, she'd know what to do with it, never let any mere woman cut off hands and feet, and legs and arms and all the rest!

The English comic strip smile of self-satisfaction says, "I've got mine. And you don't." The American's winsomely innocent smile says, "I've got mine. And you love me for it."

Tender awe. Tenderness in awe of itself. What this touches it calls "sacred."

Beyond "testing the limits," the misbehaving child is testing the limit beyond all limits – to experience the thrilling, ultimate adventure of punishment: his non-existence and "the little puff replacing him."

There are no fans on the field – and no players in the stands.

In the Classical view, a suffering king is still a king suffering. Romanticism adds a measureless pathos: his suffering empties his history, breaks down his rôle – now his suffering is nobody suffering who suffers being, suddenly, nobody.

49

A large fact of social existence doesn't speak its name because it doesn't know its name: humorlessness.

Le vice bourgeois: social self-flagellation (though there's no lack of willing hands to help).

Pillow talk, with its slow, musical musing aloud, is the true conversing couples miss in their daily, agenda-driven jousting.

Unlike bad faith, candor is lighthearted.

Tactless where most needing tact. People, confessing at long last, are so carried away by their flight into truth they disregard their audience – as if their urge to speak must supervene anyone else's wish not to hear.

Jack and Jim are fortunate to be each other's rival, since neither has any other.

A mystery how affliction confers authenticity, miraculous powers, sacredness on the afflicted one – *"powerful with what rejoiced, destroying him."* Scars, bent back, hollow cheeks, twisted limbs, blind eyes: these are the god marks of the god presence.

"Elegant sorrow?" Looks good on paper. And underneath? Wreckage, powers of affection crippled, heart's squalor.

"If he treats *us* like this, think what he'll do to our enemies!" Rush Limbaugh's *ditto-heads* adore their champion, and recognize his power's implacable authority in his complete contempt for them.

After his small success: his sweet, little swagger. Ah, he knew immortality before immortality knew him.

To keep something safe a man makes it big enough to be its own bulwark; a woman makes it so small she can hide it about her person, in her body.

All those associated with the king spoke as executors of the royal will. Ministers and their underlings were no longer persons in their own right but servants who paraded the livery of the House of Bush.

Say what we like about layers of the onion, it is still onion all the way through.

Conscience may be harsh because, poor thing, it is a solitary haunting the margins of the mind. Be kind, speak to it, bring it into the human circle, where it may learn to live among people.

Here is the brave talk of "self-renewal" and there – left behind but not left behind, since they will accompany you – are the broken lands, the psychic costs of failure, of fragmentation.

Each lie is terrible, but, worse, taken together, they are truth's new standard. Who now believes anything that doesn't ring true like a lie?

Beyond his criminality, the thief suffers from his failure to add value with his theft; not an outlaw only, but also sterile: the thief is a metaphysical neuter.

A crucial point comes when you understand your ambition should not be outside a work pushing it ahead, but inside and making it grow.

Why, when we hurt people, aren't they comforted by the knowledge they've been hurt by quite a good person? Unfair of them – and, obviously, they resent having been hurt by someone maybe a little too good for them. That's what they really can't forgive.

Prey thinks predator the dreadful, the terrible *Other*. But predator knows prey's a strayed part of himself he means to take back right now. "Come here," he says, "my lovely, myself!"

On the lip of predator's maw, prey agrees, "It is so. I was never me. And now I am coming home."

Too late he realized everything he did and said was being tested: for his strength, for his constancy. Can she count on him today? Yes? And *tomorrow?*

52

Your material resists you; your material supports you. Honor it.

In cities, it is startling to realize: everything is someone's, everyone has something.

While the self-intimidated knit their brows on the threshold, the lucky ones – too cocky and dumb to know the odds and the arduousness – walk in and make themselves at home if only in the anteroom to the vestibule.

Feeling is primordial in bringing us news of the world. And art, down to its humblest, mundane moments, renews feeling, makes it lively and fresh.

Lust undresses. Romance dresses.

The fashion for psychologizing has meant that no phenomenon suffices without its explanation, or is, finally, other than a shadow play of its reasons why.

Beyond an occasion's anger, rage arises as the effort to rectify our relation to reality or reality itself.

My immortality. Even in the grave I will turn the tables and revise my *vers*.

Companionship. A pat on the back as big as Being.

"Go ahead, you can always get divorced." So, to her daughter who asked her blessing, she offered – free of blaspheming expletives or dire prophecy – her wan curse.

The primal act of composition establishes the underlying kinship of strangers.

Whatever retreat from it may be affected, once the brink appears, it will return again and again – until someone jumps.

A line of verse is a magnifying glass in which a miniature, being deeply examined, is vastly expanded.

Moral understanding requires us to reinvent the wheel over and over again – which, though never original, is, having rolled on, never not new.

The music of a poem nails its thought into your bones.

Boys live by danger: danger defied, danger fled, danger vanquished. Respite from danger.

Custodial institutions are like families: they run on gossip.

Outsiders passing for insiders glibly pronounce the purpose of art is to shock – and confirm thereby their status as outsiders.

Shock is, in fact, incidental to the artist addressing, as he must, his immediate audience: fellow artists, who aren't at all shocked.

We keep telling the children we love them because, children ourselves once, we knew how dangerous giants are, and lived at the mercy of their whim.

Friends needn't fall in love. This violence is required to overcome inertia and the dread of strangers who are being summarily moved into intimacy.

One on whom fame was not wasted: bragging, he brought fame to fame.

In the personals ads, women's lies are adulterated with their wish to create a love-world where they fall in love with their loveliness. Their lies lack the whatever-it-takes purity of men's lies.

So long as there is one man left, this will be a man's world. The women won't have it any other way.

Nemesis is powerful because it has so many tongues egging it on, so many hands helping.

Suppose Anna Karenina, falling before the train, fell clumsily – not Anna but something in the grip of gravity – and her sacrifice proceeds beyond her power to surrender.

We know big fish eat the little fish. But the little fish, what do the little fish eat? *Themselves* they eat, fresh from big fish's gut.

Praise is never so measured there's not enough for the praiser to share in the praise he lavishes.

We are as intelligent as the information our feelings bring us.

After gripping the wheel hydroplaning 400 miles in heavy rain, he was unable to fall into sleep that night until, finally, he let the car go into an endless, terrifying skid, and he crashed. *We keep our appointments with fate, even if fate does not.*

"How will historians to come remember me?" Brazen, our leader ponders his "legacy" in the mirror of our faces. Why wait, sir? We'll tell you right now: One who made those in his care fodder for his fame. Our nakedness is what your vanity will wear on your long jog into night.

How shall minnow pass for whale? Puff himself up with self-deprecation. Of course, this will be minnow-sized self-deprecation.

Fiction presents a revelation-world in whose luminous transparency, and without yielding up secrets of his own, the reader bathes and is renewed.

"Our Fiduciary Responsibility To Our Stockholders." So their Jolly Roger unfurls its legend on the dancing wind. And they plunge ahead gaily, forced, on pain of prosecution, to exert their conscienceless greed.

Shelley's "unacknowledged legislators" remained so until the honors were passed around, after which they became *acknowledged functionaries.*

Assuming the high moral ground theirs by natural right, our lords and leaders, to complete their empire, busy themselves conquering the low moral ground.

Value can only be asserted, and so enacts the miracle of making something out of nothing, of making nothing something.

Each one hides away from his human circle a tiny bubble of life to tide him over in death – while, as one of the human circle, he joins his voice to their chorus demanding of every other, *Give us back what we lent to you! We are the source and sum of life, and everything that is life is ours.*

Sheltered under big bullies, little bullies grow savage.

Rapturous the times we bestow our withheld life on others and, for those moments, make our belovèd or our child immortal. Then we bask in our handiwork. Love gone past, we again are misers of immortality.

Young, we trust our passion to spare us the consequences of our bad habits.

The liar isn't made whole by being believed.

"Why do you love me?" Flattered, he lets descend on her his litany's sweet balm: Darling, you are thus and so and so more and so most! What she means is, What do you intend for me? How will I fit in? What of myself will I use? And, yes, she has her answer.

Contrive a life through which you move unchallenged – and because no voice demanded, "Who goes there?" you are unable to say who goes here.

As with every spiritual achievement, credulity must be earned – through the labors of obedience.

Jealous, he rushed to kill before his jealousy, returning to love, should in its turn betray him.

Every legacy bequeaths death among its goods.

The seducer learned his craft in the arms of the first one who seduced him – to whom all his subsequent seductions are his vengeful tribute.

Taking things one day at a time, letting go, moving on: not to have his heart broken, he makes it as tiny as the future he feeds it.

The misanthrope is affronted by the physical presence of other persons. Not so the conspiracist who lacks, seemingly, a sense of smell: nothing repels or, in his fluid universe, makes him pause. For him, no circuit grinds to a stop or breaks, but lifts into wider, higher, shorter circuits in a world wholly a world of words.

His struggle with his material makes the maker.

Solipsists, like bad lovers, summon us to be "the substance in their self-caresses."

Confessing in public, we mask our shame by declaring ourselves not ourselves; no, we are representative, we are others. "Take me, for example," we announce, glib, preening, out-brazening our embarrassment.

Her childhood's charm lay in knowing her existence on sufferance would end when she was grown. Grown, she knows existing on sufferance is her fate.

Praise famishes, its empty calories so quickly digested. "More! More!" the diner demands. Back in the kitchen, the chef is happily licking his fingers, savoring the dish he served up and didn't have to eat.

A tourist grows "ugly" when, ill at ease, his theatrical nonchalance means to convey this alien turf is his familiar place where he's been at home just ever so long.

In the grave's factory of fungibility a nihilist finds his heaven.

The law-abiding see law everywhere; lawbreakers once in a while run across a cop.

"Talking points" are created not so much to persuade others as to spare the likeminded the embarrassment of having nothing to say.

Up to a certain speed, we accumulate Being; faster than this, carried away, we expend it.

"Pure poetry" isn't poetry purged of meaning but meaning purified of rhetoric's pressure to persuade. To approach *"la condition de la musique"* isn't to aspire to nonsense but to perfect sense, without the deadweight of moral striving and its pathos.

More viewers brighten the view. Looking creates light.

In knowing a thing you make it a creature. And any thing you know knows you.

To be like the Phoenix. To find the fire that nourishes.

The man who's imagined himself king is as rare as the woman who hasn't deeply pondered her queenship.

Mother had no birthday, and so, like the world, always was.

We create distinctions to prove to ourselves our time is not devoid of distinction. Lost from the calendar and black the year no awards were given, no honors bestowed, no prizes won.

With every change in my civil status or social condition my right to exist, my license to live, is amplified and renewed; the world punches my ticket. Failure wants to tear it up.

Listen! Do you hear the listeners, the rich quiet of their attending?

Self-righteousness is moral boasting, and no boast lacks for its lie.

The precision with which the human animal calibrates its success or failure is a matter of wonder. Nor is it less wondrous for being often incorrect.

Witness a person's loss of face, failure, ruin; suddenly, you might be a predator watching weakness make him anyone's prey. Revulsion – at him, at yourself – has you look away. But tragic art keeps you looking so his unredeemable suffering may be redeemed, in your suffering, in you.

One learns in reading the world to distinguish between signs, which signify, and selves, who do not. For conspiracists, all selves (except the ultimate, designing Arch-self) are signs, and the world is read as a text rather than seen as commingling selves and signs.

If everything is part of a plan, then nothing is itself.

Too pathetic to punish; too awful to forgive – one wanted only for him to go away.

The moment each one thought, "I raise my hand against him because he's just asking for it" – was the moment that ended the tyrant's reign, when his overreaching betrayed his weakness.

Not to see himself seen, he dons a black veil, and confesses without embarrassment, since guilt may be expiated, but, inescapably vulnerable to every knowing eye, shame is forever.

She was more indispensable to his stream of feeling than he was, and he would more easily have suffered his destruction than her loss.

Metaphors are more than linguistic, are monsters, rich evidences of life forms suddenly uncanny in their intermingling, and ready to make more astonishing life.

The charm of players warming up, tootling and scraping scales in abrupt, broken off flourishes; dancers' baby steps, half turns, taps, curls, hops; guys tossing the ball back and forth: such deep, impromptu meditations.

Misanthropes are irascible because the world is too much with them; wholly extraverted, they lack inner refuge.

Don't go to the vampire for transfusions.

One tries, sentimentally, to reenact in full knowledge what one enacted before there was anything to know.

Intimacy with others permits us to become intimate with our otherness, which is to say, their experience of us.

"If we win over the insurgents, and if we rebuild in Iraq …" That was a time when "if" was uttered with such fervor it became existential, for how could reality not crumble before their clamorous hypotheses?

It takes a knife to interrogate a live clam; a dead one just opens up.

Bird-like, the crumb she picks up frightens her, and she flies off, dropping it.

The fundamental ideals of mind are richness, and freedom.

Hard to tell where the creature ends and his turf, his context, begins.

It is sentimental to believe a truth truer for being a stark truth. There is always a richer truth to be imagined.

Fill his palm full enough, the beggar will show you the back of his hand. *Thwap!* That will teach you to think him a beggar!

Confusion! is the great Biblical curse. A sense of being out of place, or not knowing your own mind, or of things being not quite right or quite real: such the subtle echoes reaching us from tumbled Babel.

Some buck to throw off their burden; others love to strive against the harness.

The prophet is a satirist who violates the compact exempting company present.

Dad laid down the law. Mom taught dad how to act.

When, miraculously, it takes barely two words to tell you an entire world-view, the Zeitgeist has spoken in you.

"Tell us about … you know, that one." Saying it again, falling into step, calms them, listeners and storyteller alike: facts disappear in the telling, and, humanized, the world out there is the voice in anyone's ear.

In our video age, no self-respecting witch will fly without first perming her broom.

Not treated as an end but as a means, he responded as a means in a world of means: with no end in mind, but resentfully, vengefully, violently.

Authority is diminished when it displaces itself. The throne that elevates also keeps the king from moving. Static, he embodies, beyond actual power, the boundlessly powerful idea of power.

Favors received, due, overdue, returned, return pending; obligations; duties; fibs, and so forth; debts forgiven, written off, still viable; items starred, crossed out, items resurrected; gotten the better of by, got the better of: the soul withdrawn to its secret lair, totting up accounts.

Professionals value only the opinions of their peers.

The "Pottery Barn rule" according to George W. Bush: "If I break it, I break it some more."

The people's true betrothed wasn't their Leader but *his* leader, Fate: this head, so young and so dire, always beside theirs on the pillow at night.

Pantheism was possible when, down to its smallest detail, nature was benign. Now the planet is befouled, pollutant colludes with pestilent, and we Pan-diabolists tithe our crud to the Devil.

Not yielding but yielded, as if she submitted not to him but, time after time after time, to her yielding.

Insinuating, peremptory, seductive, commanding, feeling out your most hidden wish, holding their hot slogans to your throat, the mugger messages come at you in the street with "Give it to us! Give it to us! Your wallet, man! Your soul!"

Hitler set the bar for anti-Semitism so high every lesser anti-Semite crawls gratefully under it. And today's racists take shelter in the shadow of yesterday's lynch mobs.

"There's more bloodshed now? Ah, but this is just as we predicted." And so, although there was more blood, it was somehow less blood.

For the dying laureate, the state had standing by a "complimentary ambulance." Oh, yeah. Pimp my hearse! Comp my death!

The future is another country – ruled by whom we don't know who must be placated we don't know how.

Powerful, he needn't be strong; powerless, she can't be weak.

Do women in fact experience their desires as "needs," wishes so inarguably, uncontrollably peremptory they can bear no responsibility for them – and are as much their victims as you who must attend these "needs?"

Celebrity is fame still fresh. It brightens and renews the moment; wherever it visits is a party.

The grim ecological prospect shrinks the world. The future comes closer – and appears smaller.

About her little girl's small enthusiasms a mother worries that "She's getting off track." About her son's she smiles, thinking, "This will keep him out of trouble."

Much of what passes for "thought" is simply cerebration in the presence of a topic.

Wineglass in hand, Keith, celebrating, is himself a living toast held high and offered to any thirsty god in need of a splash of blessing.

The conspiracist's enlightenment darkens the matter of the world, of whatever cannot be manipulated by mere allusion.

In famously declaring he'd looked into Putin's eyes and seen Putin's "soul," Bush was extending his feudal largesse. "I hereby put you up for membership in the Club of the Good Guys, Pootie, old man. I know you won't let me down."

Knowledge is bliss, and complete knowledge (of whatever world however minuscule) is the highest bliss – and satisfies the condition of mortality: life after its attainment must be superfluous.

She says, "Back then I still had my ideals. No sacrifice was too much for me. I was strong. I felt everything."

When the instruments of criticism and analysis grow too powerful, they turn persons and art works into illustrations of their efficacy and proof of their correctness.

To speak of "evil" is not to speak of something extremely bad. "Evil" denotes what is beyond our power of explanation and gift of sympathy. Explain the evildoer or find in him a least glimmer of good, as sympathy must, and he has invaded and polluted you, and left you outcast from yourself.

Conveyor belts, wheels, pulleys, lathes, millers, routers, gears, grindstones, drill presses, resistances, projections, introjections, regressions, reaction formations, sublimations, fixations – all busily processing "traumas" into "symptoms" and "symptoms" back into "traumas." Freud's Unconscious was a factory floor in the Age of Industry.

Its interpretation is a tale told by the story through another teller.

Froth collapses under its weightlessness.

His discourse was a cloud of significance in search of a thunderbolt of meaning.

She wished to be conquered – without being vanquished – that they together should celebrate her conquest.

Even in Eden, Eve, to learn what worm of loss the future hid, vexed the present into hissing signs.

Pedestrian, you say? Yes, and with a moralizer's squeaky shoes.

Speaking less to one another, they have less to say.

Many a "lone wolf" is only a lone sheep his flock has lost.

Do children sense their molesters mean to keep them from growing up, from becoming moral centers, from developing moral depth – like the molesters, who haven't grown up?

Too small to generate value, children grow large with messages they carry, errands they run for the king and for the queen.

"Eloquence" belongs to public speech. Where intimate speech is eloquent – even in a tête-à-tête – other heads and other ears crowd the private place.

How many years of defeat and for how many deaths had he controlled his tears that, finally, he would weep in victory?

The common ceremony of our era: Outrage is anointed by levity.

We enter the world in debt to our forebears, debt we discharge with the new child we give them.

The Buddha's precious atoms circulate among the storm-blown, poisoned molecules high above the Himalayas.

In the grip of a bore, one quickly loses confidence in reality.

Praise is a poor substitute for understanding.

Quitting her older lover, she felt joy rush in her limbs. Now she was free to outlive him!

The hit-and-run lover returns along with the ambulance to murmur in your ear, "Don't worry, darling, I'm here for you."

Yes, I pardon you, but – because, offended
and aggrieved, I have been set above you
and made to be and to seem in the right
– I ask you, First, please, forgive me.

The lie within Bush's boastful "The Decider" was his panicky dread of having to stop and think.

After her eloquent self-defense, the accused threw herself on the admiration of the court.

They are everywhere, saying what is what, stepping between us and ourselves: the managers of meaning.

An infinite number of the things of which he is unaware may be said about a person – but we know him only to the extent we know what he knows.

Denied – or failing to invent – opportunities for playacting, the soul sickens with boredom.

She knows her immaculate strength – of dedication, of devotion – her unique power to make precious, to make worth beyond worthiness. She knows she is ignored where not despised. And she lives with this bitterest knowledge.

What students principally learn are their teachers: knowledge embodied, thought experienced, subtle differences of priority and emphasis, personal attestation, enthusiasm, persistence, courage; and dangerous to attack. Learning at a distance makes the same sense as raising a child "at a distance."

The spectator senses his fundamental inanity: looking on creates no value.

North and East and South and West: forefathers who from farthest away convene their powers around my empty page.

Son follows father into suicide, not to abandon the one who abandoned him – because, he knows, father is playing hide-and-seek where in his secretest hideout he waits for his boy.

The whisperer attends more acutely to his whisper than the speaker to his speech. The latter's voice fills his head; the whisperer inhabits the ear he addresses.

The violative inseminations of rudeness.

Praise her to the skies, and, however minute it may be – oh, unbearable wafting, oh, burdensome Heaven! – she will sniff out any least obligation your praise imposes.

Praying, he hears his words concentrate and magnify in the god's listening, god he overhears hearing him, and coming always closer in their common listening.

At what point do "substitutes" become "replacements," no longer fill in for the missing ones but cavort in their place for all the world to see as the new "originals?"

Age knows one season.

The challenge is to hear every moment's cry of every life: "I want to be. I bet myself."

Rudeness is the mark of the tyrant in each of us.

In the Bush administration, torture came to be regarded a sport. Olympian Donald Rumsfeld by his own reckoning took gold in Extreme Standing.

Sometimes praise is just the lash playing nice.

Rules, in concentrating the game, magnify the power of the players.

Burdensome authority always demanding we help it uphold its good opinion of itself – opinion it requires to mask its endemic precariousness.

The great ones measure their greatness by the number of those they banalize
to a vagueness of background, dim
screen for the flagrant cinema
of their bright heroic figures.

"Passive-aggressive, come out and fight me fair and square," cat calls to cowering mouse. So bully, adding insult to injury, assaults the weak for being, as weakness will be, sly.

Punishment cannot be refused, though mercy may be.

Style is like obsession in continuously making its world over as itself.

Defenseless his body exposed to the jackals and the elements, the man who's failed to dig his way into mortality; shallow his grave, the man who has no son to bury him.

Set the grotesque among rocks and trees, rivers and animals, and it is at home in the fellowship of nature.

Before a silent film, the viewer thinks, "I hear nothing. I must listen harder." And his intentness makes the seeing more acute.

To survive was ignominy, as if we were so worthless we could be offered up for adoption to Accident, which henceforth was to be – without legitimacy, without forebears and heirs – our entire family.

"Rage, rage against the dying of the light," son rages at his dying father to save his deathward son.

By the time the rebels from the North fought their way to the resorts of the South, their Kalashnikovs were beaten into Canons, and their dusty camo bloomed fantasias of palm trees, argent moons and daiquiris.

Their conversation had entered a marvelous labyrinth where there were no dead ends and every tangent led back to its heart.

Souls sold to the Devil are damaged goods. Not to worry. The Devil isn't cheated: he pays up with second-hand life. This whole business is depressing.

The pin he fashions accommodates one dancing angel, and guess who *that* is.

Tossed a few crumbs, he makes of them his Miracle of the Loaf.

Lest his profound impersonality be compromised by your personal response, the comedian hurries away to the next joke.

The creature in us feels any criticism or correction – though kindly intended, and gently delivered – harbors a wish for his death, who will have to be reborn at least a slightly different *himself.*

The finish line rushes at you faster than you run toward it.

Laugh at yourself, and the world laughs with you.

Women and warriors have dainty natures, living or dying by their morale.

At the periphery they push eagerly toward the center where the closest are falling back in horror.

How incalculable it must be, the least glimmer of the smallest hint of the first spark glowing in the resurrected body.

When making doesn't yield reality, our last hope is destruction will.

Ordered to do what he intended to do, then not he but an intruder did what he was doing.

Legitimacy is such a tender thing, so easily lost, and once lost the illegitimate authority, no longer at home in itself, feels the loss, and adds desperation to its coercions.

Believe in me, we cry, that I may believe in myself!

We inflict awe on ourselves, crave bosses and create bullies, hoping to wreathe the smeared harrow with the harrow's own afflicted blooms.

Joy is recovered innocence.

Terrible when a person's sense of intimacy with himself becomes deranged.

The comic spirit offends only when it is impure.

Cynics learn one thing so well it prevents their learning anything else.

Children of change, our birthright is skepticism
– total and unearned, but paid for afterward.

Teddy prefers his brag to your praise, the former so expertly tailored, the latter at best never quite the perfect fit – not, that is, until Teddy snips and stretches it to suit his enchanted tongue.

Our shallowness saves us from the knowledge of our shallowness.

We open our eyes and the world is light,
a radiance that opens our eyes.
As each of us has dreamed it,
so it is now in the sight of all
— cordial and plain and total.
Why waken here if not in greeting
to the embassy of everything?
Dreaming, I knew it would be so, but not
how like my dream, how truly known, how glowing.

How richly a savory put-down fills the mouth! Yes, here's the cake one eats and has, too.

A man's world? Well, men don't need to be needed; women do.

In a time of self-advertisement, people are shamed for their modesty.

The isolation of not feeling understood can craze us with fear.

Testing the extent of his Fool's license to say anything, the shock jock spouts the taboo word while claiming the free speech a large society grants — within which the ancient rule of small groups persists: Blasphemy ain't funny. Ostracism exacted, enacted.

"If all you have is a hammer, every problem looks like a nail." Pardon me, if my problem is to cut a board, my hammer looks like a saw.

The slowed movements of the pregnant women seemed ceremonious, as if they lifted or carried or set down, stepped off, leaned out and, at the same time, pointed to each gesture, offering it up to contemplation, their movements both means and ends, actual, in time, and ritual, out of time – in what figures as existence perfected.

What boy doesn't dream of being mascot to a team of gods?

Too much evidence loaded on too tenuous a thesis: camel breaks straw's back.

Routine reveals the grain of life.

Any human circle – a family, say – expands in self-sufficiency to fill its world completely. And whoever goes away it will deem its emissary in other worlds.

The final irony is that irony takes its strength from the strength of what it is unable to ironize: the power of spirit that creates value, including the value of irony.

His stupidity is clever enough to impersonate all the vices.

Teams, with their specialized and complementary skills and duties, are world constructions, their games world animations; their empty stadia are gaping graves where worlds have gone.

Before there were words, there were names. Not classes of things, but beings. Poetry means to recover the world before words.

A "little" this. A "bit" of that. You hear it everywhere. Public discourse sweet as baby talk. And, yes, a little bit of a little bit of helps the shiv go in.

On the field after the game: the mêlée of opponents embracing old teammates and friends, while, high above them in the stands, fist fights break out among the fans.

Beggar, bag lady, the homeless man with a baby carriage: the children lose themselves in wonder, staring at these completed destinies – who show life takes children this far, and then abandons them in the street.

There is celebrity's impoverished fame: a "name rehashed in rumors, face a pixel porridge" – and spendthrift fame: the moment's big man surrounded by pals who grow famous, too, in his company.

If we remember the dead, they will not forget us.

A moment's inattention: a moth-hole bitten clear through the fabric of life. Hold it up to your eye, and see out to the end of nowhere.

Where is it, the line between acceptance of everything and consent to injustice?

Tom declares his Faith in Man. Others prefer their fairy tales with animals in them.

Plain, bald-faced inauthenticity is encountered less frequently than heartfelt inauthenticity.

We hire professionals to stand between us and Trouble; and they're happy to comply: no trouble for them since it's no Trouble of theirs – nor will Trouble, they know, take it personally because, after all, they're *professionals.*

Messiah is belated, tarrying in every doorway, praying to each reluctant heart to consent to forgo its bitter privilege, its grievance against everything. Yes, I think I hear him, next door – or two doors away.

How to possess for a single instant all one's resentment claims – then give it up, give it back, give it away, have done with it forever?

Sit love down to an empty table. Salt it eats, if salt is all there is.

And all we shall know of apocalypse
is not the shattering that follows but
brittleness before, the high mindlessness, the quips.

The sensitive ax weeps – and, weeping, bites the tree.

The law of old age: Make yourself useful – or start apologizing.

Gash black in the heart of Being:
the secret fissure where the whips are kept.

Who hasn't hoped to be more famous than death?

The common thief settles for your money; the great one demands
you fork over your admiration and your – dig down deeper, man –
your gratitude.

The passivity that ends in complicity began as moral frozenness –
clotted shock, repugnance, fear – in the face of the evil act.

The ring tenderly offered, the engaged couple, their faces awestruck;
or, before the front yard's white picket fence, father and soldier son
home from war embracing: intimate moments trampled under the
crowding actors of a thousand commercials being *you* so much better than you can ever hope to be, although you are learning.

If master hands you the whip he expects you to beat yourself.

Unlike the masses, the mighty do their looting *before* catastrophe strikes.

Precocity was his advantage before it became his doom. It outgrew him by leaps and bounds. He would never grow up.

Impassive and frivolous, mineral indolence deeper than self-love: our moral inertia won't budge an inch though it cost us everything.

Old heroes ponder their wounds while all around them snotnoses crank the awe-machine.

While a work moves forward it will carry tons, but should it halt a single instant, a straw breaks its back.

You and I pay for the lies we get; rich men get the lies they pay for.

Libertarians, who should be happy-go-lucky, are angry, less at what-ever might shackle them than at what they deny themselves – the freedom to be kind.

A deck of cards. All the individual identities and values packed to-gether in darkness radiant with possibility.

Any taboo creates, beyond its single prohibition, whole zones of devastation.

A tragic hero suffers for his hubris. But what of the hero whose hubris his flatterers have thrust upon him? Perplexed and victimized by the visitation of grandeur, this fool is incapable of suffering – and others must, tragically, suffer for him.

The commonplace has it no one would write if he didn't believe his writing would somehow at some time be read by someone. This seems not to be the case with works of visual art, perhaps because they aren't acts of communication but pieces of world.

The unwelcome gift is received as punishment.

My pain takes pleasure in your pleasure in my pain. So, thanks.

The secret sharer of every secret is death.

What I know I more truly know in making it known to you.

Speak ill of the dead, and they will in their after-world speak ill of you.

Pain: the "indwelling alien."

The younger son doesn't dream of replacing the father, only of being treated no worse than his older brother. But, his father replaced, who would enact the justice he craves? That older brother? Horrors!

An artist's perfectionism drives him to cut imperfection away not as a flaw but as a piece of death.

The artist's is a practical activity dedicated to making an ideal object.

The Six Words of Happiness. "No one can blame me, because *I'm Doing The Best I Can.*"

They're not predators, the men watching the little girls grow into big girls, they're farmers.

Suffer with the sufferer, then find his strength and tend to *it.*

"Men fall in love with the deer they see in a woman," Ortega y Gasset wrote. And women? Women fall in love with the nest they see in a man.

His lies isolate the liar; his bonds with any person are fictive.

"You don't have to change. You please me just as you are," her kiss was telling the frog.

Discovered in his lies, he appears pitifully or excitingly vulnerable, self-ostracized in secrecy, having broken his ties with the tribe. He is the stranger in their midst.

Along with counselor, confessor, poet, fool, the wise king maintained among his retinue the Royal Bore – so that he might, each time he dismissed him, savor to its fullest the sweetness of life.

More than her body, more than her yielding, the seducer desires her desire – to accompany him in his solitude of desire with a vision of himself as he was when long ago, seduced, he knew for the first time desire.

Being "in the know" dooms you to know nothing but your knowingness.

There is no charm without kindness.

Not to be left behind, with powerful strokes the swimmer in his pond paces the great liners plowing up emerald tons of the wave-tremendous sea.

The artist's task is to (in both senses) *sustain* inspiration.

Pity the racist, enslaved to his shackled mind. Pity the anti-Semite in the ghetto of his shrunken soul.

Trying always to get into time with the course of things prepares you at the last for Earth's thick arm over your shoulder and your slow dancing together.

The hunter's game is somewhere over the hill; the gatherer's no farther off than his hand.

Pitied, he believes the one who pities him revels in patronizing pride, while the latter – weakened by the weakness to which pity joins him – fearing he, too, has become pitiable, hardens his heart and withdraws into resentful scorn.

When a liar tells the truth because only the truth will do, it is simply another way to lie.

Whoever propounded the notion that Don Juan was a "latent homosexual" was an overt idiot to launch this canard that women can't fascinate.

"Latent anything" seemed like a bad intellectual joke or power grab – until they began proposing laws to jail "latent criminals."

Leaving childhood's Eden and gazing from its threshold at Everything, adolescent Adam finds himself overwhelmed with world-weariness.

Emesis is not catharsis.

So proud of them she rushes home with the news – to have him join her in admiring her brilliant reasons for dumping him.

Scraps of luck I save up. Leeways I give myself. My meannesses. My sneaky envy. Damage I can do if I have to and then I don't. And "Hey, I'm just as good as you!" Self-kit, be with me when I'm in the street, and nobody knows who I am.

His self-denial enables the leader's authority – whose mystery any self-indulgence makes ordinary. Then, no longer matching the self-denial it imposes, his power declines into brute force.

The reward ("Yes, here it is. It's coming true again.") reinforces. Then the reinforcement rewards. ("Yes, I was right. Just see, it all makes sense.") So, for the conspiracist his endlessly rewarding en-lightenment comes to replace the world.

The will-o'-the-wisp of translators: to bring the "music" of the orig-inal poem over into the new language. But this "music" isn't aural, it is semantic, and takes its meanings from its place within the range and practices of its language. Sound for sound translation is as meaningless as word for word.

Do the goodhearted advocates of "empathy" understand its most vivid, powerful, even predatory form is *envy?*

What is "lost in translation" is the inexplicit and unsaid in a work: the intimate and enveloping presence of its entire native tongue – which is not to be garnered in the new tongue, except over time as the work is absorbed and naturalized, and becomes a new work.

"I wouldn't marry you if you were the last man on Earth! But if you *were* the last man on Earth, it would be all right for you to be my dad."

Because of its harmonizing power, we can speak of the "music" of attending.

At any event, the responding audience's higher pitches predominate. It's the women feeling on holiday and alert to everything.

Its written text is the poem in exile, and waiting to be brought home by being voiced aloud or half-aloud or silently.

Sympathy is not so easy for the second as for the third person, whose sympathy imposes no obligation.

Ungrateful? Perhaps, but not given a turn at giving put him in a rage of envy that made the gift intrusive and receiving taking. Now both rage their partnering creates no value.

Is no act complete without a witness? Man the theatrical animal.

Bearing witness, we give the dead a voice, and reclaim our right to live. Silent, blind, we are dead with the dead.

Imagination bathes the fated actuality of fact – what was and is once only – in possibility, which sets it free to live on beyond time.

Childhood's warrior ideal. Inner, laconic stillness and reserve's in-gathering of forces: compassion cannot enlist these but duty will when the boy leaps to serve the weak and restore the wronged.

Scholars like to think poets exhaustive students of their art. Rather, a poet's specific aptitude is for intuiting a world from two or three words or from a wordless cadence or a snatch of tune.

The "return of the repressed" occurs not with the sensational force of its Freudian rendering but as a displaced stranger shriveled with anachronism and badly needing immediate transfusions of melodrama.

Triumph dizzies, until it stupefies – while the losers, with everything to explain, get busy with reasons and the reasons for the reasons, and come to own their defeat far more completely than do the victors the victory possessing them.

Losing, Roy smashes his racquet, bashes his head, curses, curses, curses the day he was born. Roy, fill your mouth with praise, praise your opponent, praise him to the skies, praise him, praise him.

We are constituted to come to the aid of our fellow men. If we fail to, if we stand aside, we lose some part of our moral weight, diminish our moral standing. We know it in our bones. No bystander is innocent.

Little place. Enormous horizon. The romance of islands.

Just seeing it makes you complicit, and if complicit, then compromised, fatally so to your ability to oppose them. The devils want you to watch.

Joe preferred regarding his legal problem as an ethical one, which he could then negotiate with himself, and on somewhat favorable terms.

He proceeds by every which way, in tangents, astray, askew, digressing from digressions, shambling, shuffling to find his thought – haystack in search of a needle.

Our thought, our inner monologue, is, implicitly, dialogue – speech always addressed to someone.

The stone in the stream says, "I may be wet, but I'm not water!"

Number him among the benevolent rapists who screw you for your own good.

Runs in the family. Just as dad sent an army to Panama to arrest a single man, son sent a larger army to Iraq to topple one – who'd threatened dad. Patricians owe themselves the dignity of taking things personally, and, employing our lives and treasure, do themselves this courtesy.

The young are befuddled and stymied by praise that interrupts their effort to win it.

Conscience, whatever its claims for itself, is not above suspicion, and requires the same vigilant inspection it enforces.

The power that corrupts the mighty corrupts the weaker as well. Mimicking the bully, they take on, within their smaller sphere, his corruption, passed downward until it infects everyone.

His first kiss woke Sleeping Beauty. With his second kiss the Prince tried to put her to sleep although she fought him hard. Oh, love was well enough, but never so exciting as using all her faculties.

Patience befriends time.

The Attorney General says, *Screw "reputation" – everything is shit because "everyone dies."* Then let iniquity avenge him on mortality. And who are we to judge? We're dead, too. The world's all one dumping pit. General Zombie governs from the grave.

Her labor was to divert his arterial spurt through a thousand capillaries – of habits, of plans, of memories – to create and sustain this being, their "relationship," her living work of art.

The space in which things are is different from the space in which things grow.

Postmodernism secretly rages at its subject matter made puny by being denied autonomy.

That she lies is a truth she need no longer savor in secret. Found out, redeemed, happily grateful, she says, "I can't put anything over on you!"

The world opens for a "promising" youth. Even those who might stand in his way step aside and joyfully wave him on toward a world they see suddenly hopeful, possible, open.

"Poetry after Auschwitz is impossible" – because everything is impossible; the world's dimension of possibility was murdered, and where it was is death.

Yes, there are poems "after Auschwitz," which are at the same time "impossible" – because, robbed of our right to exist, *we* are impossible, and yet, "unblessed, unsanctioned, foraging our own fields at night, hiding be day," we remain.

The most common and therefore unrecognized narcotic is fatigue.

Hiking in the mountains of Castile, Camilo José Cela crossed paths with a lone donkey bearing, hung from its neck, a sign reading, *Có-jeme qué mi amo ha muerto.* "Take me because my master has died." Yes!

The braggart's prime – and, at the last, his only – audience is his inner gawker gazing up at him in wonder.

As with every negotiation, his courtship provides her with the occasion and materials to court herself.

The pure, uncomplicated joy of begging for others.

From empathy we wish to relieve our fellow man of his bad fortune; by the same token we wish him not to relieve us – from empathy – of our good.

Style grapples with its opposite. Manner insists on itself.

When we're bad, its rough, abrupt awkwardness alerts us; we know we're bad. When we're good, the comforting, anodyne smoothness of being ourselves lulls us, and it is a struggle to wake from one's goodness to a larger, fresher self.

Lacking *sprezzatura,* his prose was the studied choreography of a stutterer in a minefield of consonants.

Eat or be eaten. Food lies naked before us, offered up for our delectation. So, garbed in modesty, we place ourselves on the preferred side of this division.

With prayers and praise and sacrifice, they undertook the care and feeding of God to give Him the strength and confidence to be their bulwark against a terrifying universe where everything was determined, everything was random.

Not suffer fools gladly? But he enjoys them mightily.

Immortalizing his beloved, the poet takes on her mortality.

"The Decider" didn't decide he was The Decider, he was told he was.

Arriving seemingly from beyond, the prohibition became in time, after dwelling among them, an invitation.

"I take full responsibility." With these words the cover-up began. Now everyone, relieved to think no more of the matter, returned to things as they were while praising him because "You see, he says he takes full responsibility."

Suborned to bear false witness, he said to himself, "If I don't, someone else will." Whereupon, he was someone else.

Praise appropriates. Now let the god escape if he can the clutches of our heaven-high and higher hosannas!

Food does not compete, food cooperates with teeth.

Not having first dreamed his tumult of adoration, she felt not welcomed by love but accosted by desire.

In the famous photo, Rumsfeld, Rice, Bush, Cheney striding toward us: The Four Pedestrians of the Apocalypse.

Orpheus, powerful, sings his self-manifestation. Eurydice, endlessly more surrendered, silent, dying into her dying. Which the greater feat? Whose the greater mystery?

Praise, in magnifying the god's greatness, magnifies his solitude, solitude at the last so great the highest praise never reaches it.

The clown's dignity established the stage the clown's pratfall collapsed – which dragged down, in turn, the bleachers where we sat, our dignity in splinters, our eyes embarrassed by what he hadn't, as he lay there, invited us to see. Then we remembered to laugh.

Where are the café jokes of yesteryear? They're in the classroom wagging gray beards.

Victories too easily won seem not worth winning, the adversary too trivial to have tarried over and your weapons suddenly slight, as when words defeat the world – by definition, as it were. Art lies in losing, in letting the world invade your words with its weight.

Life is possible when life is possible, when it has futures.

In the very instant he steals it, the thief robs it of value, since, purloined, the thing is orphaned, owned by no one, least of all by him. No longer a self, it is a sketch of itself.

First, the con man conned his conscience to invest in him. Now, being single-minded, he goes forth and he inspires confidence.

Civility and Solipsism. At the end of hockey series, two files of opposing players move past each other and shake hands; in baseball's parody, the losers hide in their dugout while, alone on the field, the winning team shakes hands with itself.

What would be the best interpretation of a work that matters to no one?

The extraordinary may recur, though only as performance.

After trial by fire is trial by ash.

The commandment enabling every other commandment: Pay attention!

Inklings, symbols, hints: she savors their indirection with sly surmises and subtle interpreting – until they reveal themselves savored over with *her*, and enter into her secret knowledge of everything. This explication of the inexplicit, teaching dumb gestures to speak, is a work of art – and hers.

Five words his charm labors to have her forget: *"What am I doing here?"*

"You always understand everything I say." Lovely praise … for a car, perhaps, purring so responsively there is nothing for him to understand about *it* – as she understood.

They loved one another and were good – and wouldn't have made accidental or false or copy or defective children. Because of this we know we are the very ones: unique, intended and true heirs.

Wisdom multiplies to meet the suffering available, without in any way creating a scarcity.

Pain helps even the jaded rediscover their innocence.

l by fire is trial by ash.

mandment enabling every other commandment: Pay atten-

symbols, hints: she savors their indirection with sly surmis-
btle interpreting – until they reveal themselves savored over
and enter into her secret knowledge of everything. This
on of the inexplicit, teaching dumb gestures to speak, is a
art – and hers.

ds his charm labors to have her forget: *"What am I doing*

ays understand everything I say." Lovely praise … for a car,
purring so responsively there is nothing for him to under-
out *it* – as she understood.

ed one another and were good – and wouldn't have made
al or false or copy or defective children. Because of this we
are the very ones: unique, intended and true heirs.

multiplies to meet the suffering available, without in any
ting a scarcity.

ps even the jaded rediscover their innocence.

Lacking *sprezzatura,* his prose was the studied choreography of a
stutterer in a minefield of consonants.

Eat or be eaten. Food lies naked before us, offered up for our delectation. So, garbed in modesty, we place ourselves on the preferred
side of this division.

With prayers and praise and sacrifice, they undertook the care and
feeding of God to give Him the strength and confidence to be their
bulwark against a terrifying universe where everything was determined, everything was random.

Not suffer fools gladly? But he enjoys them mightily.

Immortalizing his beloved, the poet takes on her mortality.

"The Decider" didn't decide he was The Decider, he was told he
was.

Arriving seemingly from beyond, the prohibition became in time,
after dwelling among them, an invitation.

"I take full responsibility." With these words the cover-up began.
Now everyone, relieved to think no more of the matter, returned to
things as they were while praising him because "You see, he says he
takes full responsibility."

Suborned to bear false witness, he said to himself, "If I don't, someone else will." Whereupon, he was someone else.

Praise appropriates. Now let the god escape if he can the clutches of our heaven-high and higher hosannas!

Food does not compete, food cooperates with teeth.

Not having first dreamed his tumult of adoration, she felt not welcomed by love but accosted by desire.

In the famous photo, Rumsfeld, Rice, Bush, Cheney striding toward us: The Four Pedestrians of the Apocalypse.

Orpheus, powerful, sings his self-manifestation. Eurydice, endlessly more surrendered, silent, dying into her dying. Which the greater feat? Whose the greater mystery?

Praise, in magnifying the god's greatness, magnifies his solitude, solitude at the last so great the highest praise never reaches it.

The clown's dignity established the stage the clown's pratfall collapsed – which dragged down, in turn, the bleachers where we sat, our dignity in splinters, our eyes embarrassed by what he hadn't, as he lay there, invited us to see. Then we remembered to laugh.

Where are the café jokes of yesteryear? They'r
wagging gray beards.

Victories too easily won seem not worth winn
too trivial to have tarried over and your weap
when words defeat the world – by definition,
losing, in letting the world invade your word

Life is possible when life is possible, when it

In the very instant he steals it, the thief robs
loined, the thing is orphaned, owned by no
No longer a self, it is a sketch of itself.

First, the con man conned his conscience to
being single-minded, he goes forth and he i

Civility and Solipsism. At the end of hocke
posing players move past each other and sh
parody, the losers hide in their dugout whil
winning team shakes hands with itself.

What would be the best interpretation of a
one?

The extraordinary may recur, though only

He rushed home at midnight fearing he was late for his insomnia. Not to worry. There it was, waiting up for him.

The humorless think comedy is being "funny," since, they believe, there are rules for being funny. No rules, though, for creating pleasure.

Speed of shadow is equal to speed of light.

This old gray nag, he's still what he used to be.

But of course! The morning after the campus riot, here was Leon the rapist on guard at the door to the girls' dorm.

The Big Man cries out, "Why can't I do as I please?" – indignant he doesn't simply have his way but must bribe, lie, inveigle, corrupt, flatter, coerce, plot, in other words, *work* to get his way. And then, "I am a poor man, I am a weak man if all my riches haven't freed me from these small fry nibbling at my freedom with theirs!"

Love: not to be spoken of on an empty stomach.

The painter stretches the canvas; he primes it; he waits for the primer to dry. He imbues and endows the canvas' every thread and pore with patience. The work's depth and field is patience.

The disciple's tragedy is being the wrong son, the one who wishes to copy the master, and not the one who runs away and whom the master loves and accompanies in thought as far as he can.

If you wish *noblesse* to *oblige*, know your place.

Back then, the lonely struggle to sneak its contraband truth past the Censor. But escaped to Censor-less America, Irony, subverted by freedom, went into business for itself: to make Irony the Censor.

The enterprise of Conrad's colonial freebooters in Africa is founded on lying to women. Believing in nothing, they would sink into paralyzed apathy if women – their last resource of innocence – didn't believe in them.

Poems no one reads or heeds or recalls, where do they go, the millions of them, illegible on the swart pages of oblivion's anthology?

"And they lived happily ever after" – telling over and over again the labors, despairs, the hopes, the sudden frights and adventures and accidents that brought them they didn't know how each time to this happy state.

A thing is a creature when it offers and invites a response. A creature is a thing when it doesn't.

Born in rage, they live in nostalgia for rage, and recur to rage to be reborn in rage.

To penetrate your material to the point that penetration is absorption and thought is thought embodied.

"The great thing about poetry," they say, "is that it can mean anything you want it to mean." Philistinism reduces imagination to fact and then moralizes, while Enlightened Philistinism trivializes, taking freedom of thought into the realm of mindlessness.

Some kisses are statements, some kisses are questions, some stop the mouth altogether.

Some want to win at all costs; others prefer losing in the highest court to winning in any lower one.

The more this official says he was wrong, the less wrong he becomes; the more practiced his delivery, then his faith if never good is somehow better – and history the more likely to judge him wise and right after all to have made the catastrophic mistakes he made.

Where he had anecdotes, she had stories.

It is discourtesy not to say what we truly think. It is discourtesy to say what we truly think.

In consumerist society, the sellers try to enslave the slave in us under color of offering more freedom ... of choice.

Al is so tough he's rotten with tough.

Conscience again: carping, fault-finding. I say, Silence it with *your* indignation at your failings. Then the voice you hear is your voice and not that alien invader's, that kibitzer from Mars.

Imagine the characters in a film twitching, fidgeting, craning out to catch the soundtrack's music inaudible to them – hoping to know the larger continuum in which they make sense. Imagine we are they.

Appearing always almost about to engage while in fact excluding you – such is this bore's cunning craft.

Let a teacher point out, however gently, a work's defects, and the inert student mindset rouses to rococo ingenuity to defend it – as if to rescue a damsel in distress from critics (big, bad, vulpine), and thus preserve the students' innocence and the world's goodness. Wisely, they refuse to grow up before they're ready to grow up.

Authority imposes by making itself difficult to please. How unlike the ethical inspiration heroes evoke.

The comedian confessed his iniquity, and the audience laughed. The joke was on him to think he would be taken seriously.

Even where unhappy, the great appeal of families is that, with their samplings of humanity, they are theaters, in which everyone is at once actor and audience and the stage is anywhere. Excruciating, perhaps, but grand entertainment not easily obtained elsewhere.

Every good poem began its existence as a bad poem.

To keep from obsessing over slights, R. adopted the motto "Don't hate. Just kill – and move on!"

Men didn't envy him his whore but his riches, for whom dropping 4,000 bucks on her was like getting it free.

We infer what danger may befall the shadow figures on a screen. Not so with a stage's physical persons whose jeopardy is immediate and inherent in their presence there, and who, bearing this danger with them, may any moment step forward and confront us where we sit.

Saith the Televangelist, "There's a sucker reborn every minute."

Fear most the lazy predator, who hunts at home.

Not to think them "little men," a woman will think them "little boys" – whose spurts of enthusiasm she may wisely guide or warily elude. What rouses her to admire "real men" is their integrity, in which she sees the self-surrender without loss of self, the idealism, the dedication she knows to be her most heroic and empowered state.

Moral authority derives ultimately from your willingness to interpose your mortal body.

In the Hell of Fame the stars and starlets cruelly outnumber the groundling eyes available to regard them.

A simple crime harms its victim. A hate crime injures the idea of his existence and that of everyone in his hated group.

Oh, he was utterly ridiculous, but, because he refused to imagine himself so, he was immune to the ridicule we lavished on him – and we, left with our heaps of useless ridicule, saw *we* were ridiculous.

"To find the extraordinary in the ordinary." Thus the re-enchanters push their inflated currency. However, finding in the extraordinary the ordinary – this is the work of the de-mystifiers, the comic souls who cool conceit and calm desire (and seldom advertise).

Florida: a game preserve where death finds the hunting good.

Do women instinctively fear men as unpredictable predators capable of turning at any moment and devouring their children?

L. defined seduction as "trying to turn a stranger into an intimate." Just like L. not to add, "Without pausing to make him a friend."

S.'s first act in perfecting his snobbery was to snub that pretentious, infinitely inferior being S.

A "passive slave" woman turns herself into a "piece of meat," saying with her silence, "How dare you call yourself a man when I'm a piece of meat? Don't feel proud of being the master of this nothing, who is a living reproach to you!" As if he cared.

Her constant companion was the tinnitus of criticism – approval, disparagement – raging in her head. Everything had a voice, and the voices, pushing and pressing, told her who she was while their un-failing pressure kept her in the world.

What drew him to psychology was wanting to know what it might be like to have a psyche.

His soul's effort to trim its craft, to balance it and haul in whatever might be dragging on its way, to be neat and plunge freely ahead, and streak off without a care in the world. So the saved soul affirms it, "Yes, I am a good boy."

Dependency is intimacy, given by taking, taken by giving.

I walk down a city street, and things are fine, okay, pretty good, smiling their approval of my presence and passage. I return their salute. A woman walks down the street; the street is vivid, sneaky, out of kilter, imminent with dangers.

"Good reasons make bad art" – not least because "good reasons" are pleased with themselves, and art their bothersome intruder.

Potter grows cool while the clay warms in her hands.

Ironizing presumes the ironist knows more about his subjects than they know about themselves. It is rude. If he must ironize, let him engage his ironic ignorance of himself, though here, too, let him be kind and, in the light of what he now knows, forgiving.

Better no poems at all than "good" poems whose goodness blights their individuality, poems good mostly for confirming the standards that make them "good."

It is happiness to be happy, but joy to make others happy. Winning, too, is good, but we are proud of the triumphs of those we love.

Priding himself on his honesty with others made him more ignorant about himself.

Conscience claims authority over me while being itself, for all I can tell, conscienceless.

Gods, too, have genealogies. And any current authority bears his predecessors' doomed legitimacy.

He calls himself a "fairly well-known writer." How do justice to the throat-clearings, the a-hemmings and a-hawings, before and after his *"fairly?"* Here is the epic soul-journey of a thumb minutely pondering its way over the scales, and pressing just *so* until the balance is struck just *there*.

Set an obstacle before the Devil, and I will root for him, though I be the obstacle.

Envy is the empathy of weakness.

Oh why
is the soul sent on errands
in the dark? with its list
of names, its fist of pennies,
its beating heart?

Rebirth doesn't change the world. No less than with birth, one is reborn into a family, a tribe, the world – all as they were when just a moment ago we left them.

Not that the Muse spurns compromise, but, precisely attuned to the ideal, she fails to register any tone not true to it.

When everything is permitted, nothing is desired.

The enduring vestige of the student rebellions was more cops on campus.

Its scientific ambitions – to establish "laws" – led depth psychology to ignore what is fundamental in persons: individual temperament. The result has been an individual psychology without individuals.

Gofer, errand boy, messenger bearing a sheaf of dispatches or most urgent word whispered in the king's ear: the person transfigured as value.

"Fire him or I quit!" Jerry's ultimatum reveals his will *in extremis,* so lacking in force he's buried it under his self's dead weight, saying, in effect, "I know I can't move you, so please move me."

Among the powerful there circulates a currency of blowjobs.

Suddenly, strangers replace your family as the arbiters of your value. For this universal passage we have no rite: our entry into the job market.

The tyrant rules by making everyone – in fact or in effect – his accomplice.

My self-satisfaction is benign, is generous: it includes you.

Suffering doesn't relieve you of responsibility to others to treat their sympathy kindly. Let your sorrows be "elegant." Learn to suffer *beautifully*, with "dignity" and with "grace."

We have set our thieves to teach us value.

Having enjoyed the game so little, his only pleasure was gloating at its end, as if his rival had all along been death.

An ironist believed his irony exempted him from the curse about which he ironized. In this wish he was helplessly sincere – and deceived, since, ironically (of course), it did not.

Each bystanding thing abides in patient insignificance; then we act, and it rouses into sudden selfhood, cheers or jeers us on our way. Everywhere we look the world is potent with danger and blessing.

Pity the poor megalomaniac. If he's not everything, he's nothing.

Mel was this kind of guy: you gave him his gift – and you ran.

Chamber music of the kitchen table; the restaurant's symphonic dining.

An idea isn't its conclusion but its argumentation.

Sympathy for the Devil. Having no place in the cosmic community of goodness, the outlaw – vivid, naked, immediate – is at every moment exposed to danger and death. And we, though faithfully companioned by our disapproval, we can't help it, we are there with him, the cosmic stranger.

No nakedness so naked it has nothing to hide.

She felt herself abstract, two-dimensional, potential without force, a statement without context, which only an attentive regard could bring to full life. She tended to her appearance, for fear she fail to appear at all.

The "Do or die!" "Now or never!" of performance makes any old work immediate and vital – even as, reading it, you whisper its words to yourself.

Just as sound creates space, listening, too, creates space, even in the absence of sound.

Vanity wants confirmation; conceit is self-sufficient.

Applause commends the players in whatever register of enthusiasm. Another, madder, applause shakes you when the play is a wilderness of forces from which not you not the players will find a way out if you don't batter your hands together beyond anything you've ever known.

Easy to amend injustice. Hard to be just.

The avidity of the strangers' stares was estranging. She was beside herself, this celebrity, fearing they'd singled her out for something terrible. She did a lot of crazy things in token sacrifice to forestall any real sacrifice to come.

Among life's disappointments: Thrilling to experience becomes tedious in the telling.

A work loses intimacy in the clamor of voices acclaiming it.

To the degree that poetry "makes nothing happen" it affirms the adequacy of the imagination, which need not, indeed, must not try to make something happen. Any trace of utility loads the imagination with the pathos of striving and the still heavier burden of failing and falling short. Whatever happens, it won't have been "made" to happen.

I may see all at once, but *knowing* what I see takes time.

The tedium of explanations: like flashbacks, they bring you only to where you all along have been.

Things dispossessed are, like orphans, incomplete until possessed again – and again are someone's asset.

Don't waste your gallows humor on the hangman, he's heard it all.

So few "get-rich-quick" schemes, so many "get-poor-slow" ones.

Envy tears the world apart; resentment brings the enviers together.

The sexter sent photos of his nakedness – to women who, desiring to know the whole man, wanted only to see him in clothes.

He was selfish and unfair. Well, had he been otherwise she'd have doubted him. She knew he loved her, because that's what love is, selfish and unfair.

For the storyteller, the past tense is an ocean of many oceans among which he moves at will, fluidly without interruption. The present tense is a staccato of *nows,* each now a now unto itself, a cell from which he breaks out – to imprison himself in the next *now.*

Critic's rule is artist's tool.

It wasn't the praise she thought it, telling him, "You're a great lover" – as if he were a professional of love and not, undone by love for her, love's rankest amateur.

Past childbearing, she was diminished by a mystery.

In his desolation of power all that connects the torturer to human-kind is scream after scream after scream.

Democratically, we are asked to "identify" with this character or that. But grant their distance from us, and we do not identify with an Oedipus, a Lear: we *behold* them. They are not to be redeemed by our sympathy, nor are we.

Their loser idea of a winner is bigly self-indulgent Trump. Whatever has been denied them and what in bitterness they deny themselves, his superb self-approval grants. They shall have what he is. And miracle, their hidden wounds are weaponized as open carry. They swagger in his brazen sun. Let everything go to hell and all shall be well!

Nihilists are proud to be nihilists.

Marjorie's was the hand that moved the fingers of Dan that moved the pen that ended his thing with Linda.

Whom the gods would mock they first make famous.

Art does not compensate for life. Art makes life more, and more intense, life – in presenting an opposing power you will wrestle, and become thereby, in whatever degree, its creature, its co-creator.

There is comfort in feeling you've been understood, discomfort in feeling you've been understood too well.

The young love "cool." Uncertain how the world they are entering receives them, they disclaim what they assert even as they assert it, coolly having it neither way.

So fascinating this froth at your lips you lose all sense of the wave hurling you down, hurling you on.

To see you as finite is to surrender you to mortality is to surrender everyone to mortality is to surrender to mortality.

For all its liveliness, the life he took would not add itself to the life he had. At his first strike, he joined his victim in mortality: divested of innocence, and his only armor now this power that each time leaves him more exposed, debt-ridden, mortal.

Skip out on your debt to X or Y, and you will discover – unburdened, pleased with yourself, skipping, no, staggering along – how at the last you are shackled to death: this creditor of creditors who holds all the tabs, who knows every score. Quick, while the till is open, pay up, pay up, free yourself and live forever!

Age turns every golden thing he touches to dross – and less than dross. They reprimand him, "Your touch is poison. You haven't time left to make anything of me. And then in no time you will take me with you."

Anticipating pain beyond bearing, he screamed, knowing that next instant it would be too late to scream.

If you had to pass a test to get into Hell, eager achievers would be fighting to be first in line for it.

Whatever its elevation or depth, his air of authority renders the pedant's every utterance a platitude.

Lionel was not so cynical he'd make use of someone for whom he had no regard. Still, when no longer useful a certain someone did seem to sink in Lionel's esteem.

In the era of the Acid Reign, the youth guru's "wild oats" was a bunch of buggered brains.

The whole is without momentum and confers this mercy on its momentum-driven parts.

This hyper-ruminant's discourse is a thrice-pulverized palaver's continuous cud of saliva and schwas.

In the rapture of their *danse macabre*, the dancers cry out hosannas in praise of Death for his leadership.

Two men, two strangers, meeting on neither's turf, size each other up. Two women bare their teeth in smiles.

When I serve myself, I am sometimes the one served and sometimes the server. I am twice a solitude … until I serve another.

"Pity and terror" slips from the tongue as if these are bound in a single pity-terror neither terrible nor pitying. But should one outweigh the other, terror disables every feeling or, terror past, pity without end sinks us in grief for who were destroyed and we lie down with them, we lie down with them.

Difficult for him to understand that because she hasn't prepared herself to feel desirable she is nonplussed by his desire, then irritated, then offended, as by something intrusively alien, for surely he mistakes her for someone – perhaps, who knows, for anyone – else!

The will is unable to act on what it perceives to be without will. So the maker instills spirit into wood block and clay lump to animate their impassivity as willfulness. They resist him … until they let him persuade them to collaborate.

Trying doesn't make it happen, but it happens only if you keep trying.

Hell is peopled by hatreds, each isolated in the prison of its arrested drama. But let a Master free them to a common hatred, and they rejoice. Then Hell is a great, collective happy hatred, a wonderful new drama, and not so bad, after all.

The words of a poem become, in their aggregate, a name: the poem names itself as an individual to be confronted and then, unlike other individuals, performed.

Ninety percent of life is conversation: with others, with others in us.

Sarcasm is rude. Still, Marvin is forgivably so, since among the humorless sarcasm passes for wit.

"After me, no other." Having scorched her heart, Joe takes it as his tribute nothing will grow there.

A poem's focus on sound transforms its words from the rawness of being heard to the intimacy of being listened to.

His generosity was exactly that and no more, since it replaced casting his lot with her. Feeling this in her bones, she demanded more and greater generosity, all the while hating him for it.

Having no audience, his speech grew more urgent, as if, for want of other ears, it would hear itself.

The true cliché's stupidity overpowers any context, and prevents its turning the cliché's truism into the moment's truth.

"No," she told her child, "I've told you twice already I won't give money to save that little child on TV." Child heard her say, "If you weren't my child, I wouldn't save *you* – so, it's lucky for you you're my child. And don't you forget it!

Giants and runts rove satire's bright precinct always rife with exaggeration and diminution. Presume to appear as you imagine yourself to be, then satire's child's-eye will delight to add you to its silly, self-blinded menagerie.

Agèd they may be, but the old are never too old to speak ill of the old.

For those who've never loved themselves enough, Jack is loving himself for you.

We admire our hero for the protection his power confers but love him for the protection his vulnerability beseeches.

It is said a platinum replica of Nancy is maintained at a constant temperature in Geneva as *The International Standard of Reason*. This I know: lie down beside Nancy and you are sure to come up – in mind as in body – a wee bit short.

Cyclops, *poveretto,* is sad. "The Greek I ate today didn't taste as good as the Greek I ate yesterday, and *he* didn't taste as good as the Greek I ate the day before."

Michael excels in moral gymnastics, maintaining, in the midst of bad faith, his staunch innocence, this center of gravity enabling each next stunning flip-flop or scampering.

Poor dead Charlie on his bier mourns his paltry gathering of mourners, apologizes his life has brought together a multitude only of not much – across which we few stragglers, lacking the comfort of abundance, stare at one another and mourn not Charlie but each his own poor, lone integer of *me.*

Being an "influence" weighed him down with himself, with, that is, his followers' inertia, what in them could not exert itself except as *he.*

Public life, this great slap-and-kiss machine; whoever enters joins the Censoriat of all of us dealing and being dealt slaps and kisses, kisses and slaps.

Fearful before your excellence, I submit and, submitting, join, and joining, possess and, possessing, rejoice in your wonder, and my adoration is powerful.

The fantasist continually revises his daydream. A story tells itself.

Creation begins as a force field of the not and the not yet. Whatever falls into it reveals itself as composable – before any composition has been imagined or struck.

Your guilt is yours. But, embarrass yourself, and I am embarrassed *with* you and embarrassed *for* you in our contagious fellowship. Guilt, being personal, incarcerates the guilty fellow, while leaving us free to go on with our unembarrassed back-and-forth about his unpleasant situation.

He joked in the comforting illusion that if you're in on the joke the joke can't be on you.

A lie refers to nothing but itself, and so exists in a nonce language unintelligible even to the liar – until the common tongue explains its purpose and restores the lie to the world of truth.

Every lie isolates the liar from his fellows and from truth, leaves him lone alien in a world of truth. Exiled monarch of his nowhere, he is vulnerable to everything.

Truth is fundamental; it connects us to one another.

They offer "fast food" to exact fast feeding.

A work cooked at too low a pressure boils off before heat can be applied.

They are old, and we no longer require their collaboration in maintaining the consciousness that is the world; the day, we feel, takes place without them. They, too, feel this.

Steven mistakes critical self-consciousness for intellectual scruple. So long as he is aware of what he says – its sources, context, implications – he feels free to say anything.

As a symbol-user, she detests the literal: it is crude, inconsiderate, disrespectful, refuses to let her bring her powers into play and even denies them – unless she can, summoning her wits, render the literal symbolic, the alien civil.

Because they failed to come to resemble one another, their rivalry was catastrophic. The loser, having neither acquired nor contributed to the winner's qualities, could in no way share in his victory – and the winner was left vulnerably their rivalry's sole survivor.

Ecstasy whose period is so long its every moment is stillness. Such is the bliss of heaven.

Independent? Of course, Professor K. is independent. He marches to the clunk of a different cliché.

When Mary came to tell the story of her life, the God part might well have been its high point; certainly, it wasn't its *only* point.

Knowing himself powerless, feeling himself inessential, the child, eavesdropping on existence, most believes what he *over*hears.

He brays outlandish, meaningless, irresponsible things, and they feel freed to riot in moral saturnalia; high on the afflatus of empty words, they rejoice in their demagogue-hero whose license has empowered them to take leave of their senses.

She emerged from adolescence sensing her destiny: affianced to Everything to give birth to the world.

Lagging behind, we begin to perceive the forward rush of existence. Our force was part of its force, and now it overwhelms us with its accusation we abandoned it – because, we know this now, it always required us to add our mite.

Men enrage her because they demand *both* comfort and glory – when she knows that, given their freedom, just one would satisfy her. (And so she thinks, having neither.)

The man who praises himself has a pauper for his patron, lacking the wherewithal to earn another's accolade.

Art stubbornly recalls us to its surface, to what is understood without being put into words.

Praise is presumptuous when it pretends to the intimacy of touch.

However singular in beauty each gleaming jewel, every next brilliant dropped on their glowing heap dulls them to a pale pile of fungibles.

The Golden Rule's Dark Underside. Because you did unto them as you did, you conveyed along with your misdeed the goodness and invulnerability of your lost innocence. You know it now: they will do unto you what you did unto them, and their misdeed will be righteous.

He offers companionship to the bereft deity who once inhabited him: loyal to the god in whom he no longer believes.

The point of the catharsis of fear and pity is to show us we have survived the worst, and so may take heart and live again.

Being wholehearted half the time won't be so easy as being half-hearted all the time.

What we found outrageous was to her just tidying up some minor mess before things got out of hand. After each lie, her smile all but invited us to admire her sparkling parlor.

Scraped strings and strummed strings. The violin's sounds were proportionate to the intensity of the player's bowing, and as such seemed *produced* sounds quivering with the effort that made them. The meandering of the guitarist's fingers let note by note drop into a meditative space, not made but listened-to.

Reciprocity not required. T. *exacts* praise, wishing to wrest it as tribute, not receive it as a gift.

The project of consumerism is to turn what was always deemed the pain of desiring into the pleasure of desiring.

How am I to recognize your moral superiority to me without being tempted to belittle morality?

How many moralizers are inspired by heroes whose names they no longer know?

Minimalism elides the artist's signature. A pristine anonymity invites you to inscribe and then to elide yourself.

You escape the mouth of the Ogre only with your own shining set of choppers.

Burning under a million gazes: celebrities' otherworldly faces. We can't imagine anyone ever having looked at them with love.

In their household's economy, the active one is happy, the busy one is busy.

Whatever its claims, the inner monster doesn't want justice, it wants to be the outer monster crying aloud, "See what you've driven me to!"

The punishment for obsession is your sense of humor locked up in solitary confinement.

D.'s air of determined mediocrity, of dumb resoluteness announces: "I will cut down to size any man I'm connected with. Let him not think he's anything special or free or has a single margin that exceeds me."

Barbara's mouth is a portrait of distaste, because, as evidence of her superiority to her circumstances, nothing could be more *distingué* than disgust.

The handball players don't cheat to win (winning is for pussies); they cheat to get their own way, cheat to have something to yell about, feel their voices fill their throats, hear it fill space, see it blast the other guys into anger. They refuse to fall behind in rage, be outdone, outshouted, outcheated – that would be dishonor, death. They love it, as proud, nervous, vain and death-provoking as warriors!

The adept of "process" goes on about the ins and outs of how he created his barely formed work, which appears to have a biography without ever quite having had a life.

Far from being envious, the fishermen on the pier are helpful, amiable, peaceful. Who would compete before the water's fluency, the ocean's wide, companionable grandeur? Who would not feel gathered together in the embrace of its magnitude?

Did the magazine makers believe the photographs of naked men would arouse women? Here is some vain guy lying there to be admired instead of – what *would* turn her on – *doing something*, making himself useful, showing he could help her realize her plans and, not incidentally, paying attention to her.

His panic was a flight toward self-concern, to where, finally, he could stop and lick his wounds.

The thief is a middleman. How, then, undersell and drive him from the market?

What the lapdog did to her lap was for a long moment warm, then for far too long a moment cold.

Small wonder each of us social animals is himself a society of selves, of selves and others.

What counts in a work isn't formal closure or openness but the movement of thought. If thought fails to go on, adventure and discover, then "closure" has taken place, whatever the formal "openness." And if thought does adventure, then formal closure is another of its adventures.

It is morally irresponsible to believe a liar, giving the lie shelter and comforting the liar with your fellowship.

Some artists wish to give pleasure. Some prefer to astonish – astonishment laced always with a dash of pain.

Mrs. Roy T. Moore boasted, "And one of our attorneys is a Jew!" No less broadminded, attorney replies, "And one of my clients is a bigot!"

The more powerful the authority, the more imperious its demand for gratitude. Subjects are to show they love the gifts the lash bestows. Only so, may the tyrant, in his isolation of power, be saved from seeking companionship in self-pity.

The dog in the manger is never so vicious as in guarding for himself what he hates – and hates himself for guarding.

Wit is impromptu, original, fresh, alert with risk transcended; wit dances with you on the brink of its moment.

Declining a divorce of her own, Wanda never discourages friends who would offer her the chance to divorce by proxy.

Innocents complain their despoilers are insatiable – who in turn and in all innocence complain, "Why aren't these suckers more *forthcoming?*"

The liar doesn't address you. He addresses the someone else you are should you believe him.

If trust in you is a contract I make with myself, how far am I to trust myself?

The "self" is dramatic: I am selfless *me* until I discover I am pitted and pitting myself against this abrupt whatever-it-is *not-me.* So salesman or seducer, not to startle customer or mark into sudden selfhood, disguises himself as *mirror-me.*

Authenticity is not self-authenticating. It may be granted – or denied or withdrawn – but only by others. Nor is any such juror credentialed "authentic" – until, that is, he renders judgment, and in and by this act authenticates himself.

It is given to most of us to be either fool or knave. Leave it to superlative T. to be both at once, never stinting on one to benefit the other. In their perfected synergy, knave fouls fool, fool fairs knave, so knave is the more fool, fool the more knave.

Two persons each know the same unspoken thing. But if they speak it aloud to one another and know it together, they make their knowledge and their knowing known to a third person, call it "the world" their witness. They have, for good or for ill, pledged their knowledge.

You can't get a piece of the action without becoming part of the action.

The Unconscious exists only in the interpretations of its interpreters, as, then, the consciousness of others.

Pegasus leaps from the brightness flaring beneath his springing hoof ignited each time hoof strikes down.

At the wedding party's climax what was meant to happen happened: Everybody married everybody.

After the techniques (for example, "how to read a poem") were applied, the old tales no longer gave pleasure or guidance. The givingness of the given had been abolished. The tales were now "texts," raw material for the newly fangled technicians. Negatives of the tools that made them, sports, never would these products live to be old tales.

Body so long held aloof has fallen into the hands of doctors, nurses, almost anyone, to be touched freely by fire water earth's everywhere.

Jack abuse Jill? *Not possible.* This body Jack lets out to her is his. It's Jack's. It's Jack's property. Listen to me: Jill's got a good deal going – it's practically free, and, hey, where else could she live? So, Jill honey, don't bitch or hold out on Jack when he comes knock-knock-knocking for the rent. You think your body's *you?* Guess again. Jack can knock it or fock it because it's *his.* 'Fess up, Jilly, you know what I mean: if not for Jack you're just another ghost out there mooing and moaning with the rest. So show him a little gratitude, not to say respect. Thinking maybe you can do better? Want to try Jim? Go on, try Jim. He's got a vacant property or two. But just you remember, Jack or Jim, whatever they own, they own it in perpetuity. That means, *forever.* So long as they want it. Okay, what the hell, I'll let you in on a little secret maybe you're starting to guess: *everyone* owns you, Jill – or whatever it is you like to call yourself.

Envious, my painful pleasure is to possess in thought what you possess in fact. Resentful, my rage annihilates its worth and heaps your precious void with my misery.

Clown invites, welcomes, embraces your smug self-indulgence. He gloats over your stupid laughing so unaware his silent last laugh is killing you.

What Four Horsemen of the Apocalypse could not accomplish one little fool does, and keeps on doing.

Form in a work of art is, most deeply, neither shape nor structure but the context of experience it invokes which then presses back on it.

130

Swindler vanishes. Savings vanish. What you have now is knowing you've been had. So, you no longer believe swindler but, to restore your vanished innocence, you more than ever believe *in* him – and in all heartfelt innocence cry out, No, no, no, he never lies!

He lies constantly. So, he is weak. But he lies shamelessly: he wants you to see him lie again and again. So, he is strong. He is your selfish hero who will never grow up and will cost you everything.

You have discovered the comfortable laws of illogic, the lovely disarticulations of the bones of thought. So thrilling now this newfound intellectual workout where you defend – against all reason – the indefensible, finding ways to help your swindler take you to the cleaners while you praise him for opening your eyes and now accepting your gratitude for all you gave and still owe him.

Give in to the tyranny of reason and be carried back into the everyday? What's exciting is this intellectual workout: finding ways, against all reason, to defend the indefensible crook, liar, short-changer, grifter who will go on taking you for all your worth. And you awake in this thrilling, promised once-in-a-lifetime no man's land where nothing means anything and fuck it all anyway – because, after all, you are worthless.

Believing lies was better than believing nothing. That was some sort of companionship.

131

Miser of his miseries, Moe is in his counting house gloating over his hoard of bad pennies.

"Deconstruction," as with *ad hominem* arguments generally, functions as the AIDS virus does, using the discourse that would deconstruct it to propagate itself.

The charm of Freudianism lay in its enabling strangers to know one another, in fact, know one another better than each knew himself.

Then Jewish identity's "Do you live as a Jew?" became "Will you die with the Jews?"

A great relief to find at last, after so many misadventures, what he had despaired of finding: a partner who was shallower than he. Now his work was cut out for him: out-shallow her.

She sees his prick, and thinks, "He has that. What does he need me for?" But: In her mind, is her body, no, is *she* the prick's proper sheath, its wholeness and grandeur, its comeliness and true measure? Without her that prick is what? Pointless. A lonely nothing.

Thousands may enjoy and admire his work, but his audience is the bare dozen, not all of them living, for and to whom the poet writes.

In the beginning of the end, each talked over the other's head – to history; looking forward to looking back, each said what each in the future will say to explain this failure they will have had together.

Who was carrying the torch? Who was tinder?
Who had the ball? the balls? the jism? the juice?
Who had it? the speck? the spark? the dough? the power?
And where was it going? Who'd have it tomorrow?
Single, disseminated, held in trust, hidden, passed on, usurped: power is irreducible, power is indestructible.

She hates the English muffin he is eating. How dare this burnt, soggy thing usurp his entire attention! And how dare he!

We know Him to the extent we reveal ourselves to Him. The spy, too, is governed by the rule: We know in so far as we are known.

The trivializers of the Holocaust aren't so wrong as the Holocaust deniers, but they're wrong enough. But then to be right about the Holocaust as if that put you in the right, that, too, is wrong. Everything is wrong.

Love follows the beloved into death to preserve the beloved's immortality there.

Waking from lies decades-long they believed, they know the truth they didn't know, but not how to believe what they know.

133

Oh, he's not done with them. Master Scammer elevates his suckers. They are Stooges, his glorious Stooges now. Recruiters of new suckers, they bolster and boost him, proud to be Master Suckers.

The actor's primal acts are entering the stage and leaving the stage. Her primal acts were affiliation and, however dire and held in reserve for use if warranted, disaffiliation.

Your overweening sympathy would deny the victim his right to refuse it – as if he were wholly "victim," not this person faced with accommodating this injury. How, then, is he to accommodate this second injury your kindness adds?

God was terse: so few words to make so much world. We, too, have few words for all this world, and yet they are words enough.

He was for a time indistinguishable from the world of feeling he awoke in her: *Loveliness and largeness and wonderment.*

Authors are a secret police. When they arrest us, they never read us our rights: "Anything you say may be written down and used in a story about you."

"He's spoiled." Meaning, "I spoil him." Meaning, "He is my handiwork."

"Such a delight for her," he thinks, "riding high on my mind's powerful steed. It gallops and bounds, prancing its joy!" But the headlong, heedless bulk alarms, and the trampling hooves' incessant battery. Years of this, and he never guesses his marvelous gift discomfits, no, bores, no, it appalls her.

Says Althea to Benjamin. "I'm getting happier now. I'm going to be good to you. Really. You'll see. I'm turning over a new leaf." Leaf so lightly turned? Not a second's penance for years of badness? Inscribed on the new leaf, it seems: Althea is to suffer being *good* to Benjamin.

Aging, he begins divestiture. Anticipating nakedness of the grave, he will, as a point of honor, not to be false to it, go naked there.

Just as power is exercised and perceived only in matters of concern, concern gives matters weight, makes them resistant, and renders power perceptible because it must do work.

When Jennifer warned me, "Just watch out. Women lie," I wondered: Thinking of their covetousness rouses her own, and the temptation to be guileful? Then, not to sink into that mass, she repudiates guile – in token of which, she offers up the rest of womankind? "See," she seemed to be saying, "for your sake, I value you so highly, I will betray my entire sex." "Thank you, Jennifer," I said very carefully.

Patience makes a moment a century, the infinitesimal infinite, the infinite intimate.

Gossip is told with the tacit proviso that it be retold. Gossip is a commodity, a secret become social commerce so long as it remains secret to someone.

Where lower classes make do with serial monogamy, the upper class has serial polygamy: harems without walls.

"I don't just envy you your poems, Gary, I envy you your *life*." Such was his fan's gushing gift: fan's disabled life swapped for Gary's great one his ardent envy all these years was feeding and eating.

Vows and devotion instill timelessness in time:
for now forever; for the time being
forever; while this lasts forever.

Joe says, "I'm back in the Church again. Going to St Jude's. I give them money. But not a lot." *But not a lot* is everything: Joe's soul offered wholly, immediately, unabashedly to God – and to us – in tentative, hesitant prayer.

We name rock tree hill lake flower mountain river, we name everything – to people the world with creatures and convene its power in ever greater societies, societies always embracing ours.

His writer's contract with the reader engages the author not to write complete nonsense. Does the reader comparably engage not to make nonsense of the work – if the reader is a signatory at all?

Apollo. Not the mind contemplating the spectacle of order, but the serenity of power in action, strength moving in matters of common concern.

Charm is a gentle ecstasy – it takes us into new worlds without demanding we leave our world entirely behind.

Only in addressing an ideal reader may he become an ideal author.

Writing this does not spare me. Nor are you spared because you read this: not pain, not joy, not the requirement to live your uttermost.

Happy endings leave you free to walk away.

Walking and talking. Dance whose music the dancers compose.

Walking and talking. Getting into time together. Nothing like it.

"And God saw that It was good." This was the second creation suffusing the world with value. And all our makings, our assertions, our very quarrels over value continuously constitute the world and out of nothing make more and more good.

We don't want to be halted by identities
– we want to go on becoming in wonder.

Acknowledgments

Selections from this text have appeared under a variety of titles in the following periodicals:

A Public Space: "Assemblage"
Antioch Review: "Engagements," "Untitled"
Hotel Amerika: "Clay Laughs"
Prose: "Mots, Motes: Extracts from a Journal"
Southwest Review: "Simples," "Simples II"
Yale Review: "Thoughts Thinking," "Usable Truths," "Reusable Truths"

For their help along the way I am grateful to: Alex and Natasha Feldman, Gail Fischer, the late Sanford Friedman, Deborah Garrison, Kenneth Gross, the late John Hollander, the late J. D. McClatchy, Don Mitchell, Cynthia Ozick, Zeese Papanikolas, Marian Parry, David Ritz, Harold Schweizer, Elisabeth Sifton and Willard Spiegelman; and, finally, to Philip Hoy for making this book.

A Note About the Author

Photo courtesy of Gail Fischer © 2004

Born in Coney Island, New York in 1928 and educated at the College of the City of New York and Columbia University, Irving Feldman taught at the University of Puerto Rico, the University of Lyon and Kenyon College before his appointment to SUNY at Buffalo in 1964 – from which he retired as Distinguished Professor of English in 2004.

He has received a National Institute of Arts and Letters award and a grant from the National Endowment for the Arts as well as fellowships from the Academy of American Poets, the Guggenheim Foundation, the Ingram Merrill Foundation, and the MacArthur Foundation.

Feldman's eleven books of poems include *Works and Days* (1961), winner of the Kovner Poetry Prize of the Jewish Book Council; *The Pripet Marshes* (1965) and *Leaping Clear* (1976), finalists for the National Book Award; *All of Us Here* (1986), finalist for the National Book Critics Circle Award; *Beautiful False Things* (2000); and *Collected Poems 1954–2004* (2004).

Other Books from Waywiser

Other Books from Waywiser

Christopher Ricks, ed., *Joining Music with Reason:*
34 Poets, British and American, Oxford 2004-2009
Daniel Rifenburgh, *Advent*
Mary Jo Salter, *It's Hard to Say: Selected Poems*
W. D. Snodgrass, *Not for Specialists: New & Selected Poems*
Mark Strand, *Almost Invisible*
Mark Strand, *Blizzard of One*
Bradford Gray Telford, *Perfect Hurt*
Matthew Thorburn, *This Time Tomorrow*
Cody Walker, *Shuffle and Breakdown*
Cody Walker, *The Self-Styled No-Child*
Cody Walker, *The Trumpiad*
Deborah Warren, *The Size of Happiness*
Clive Watkins, *Already the Flames*
Clive Watkins, *Jigsaw*
Richard Wilbur, *Anterooms*
Richard Wilbur, *Mayflies*
Richard Wilbur, *Collected Poems 1943-2004*
Norman Williams, *One Unblinking Eye*
Greg Williamson, *A Most Marvelous Piece of Luck*
Greg Williamson, *The Hole Story of Kirby the Sneak and Arlo the True*
Stephen Yenser, *Stone Fruit*

FICTION
Gregory Heath, *The Entire Animal*
Mary Elizabeth Pope, *Divining Venus*
K. M. Ross, *The Blinding Walk*
Gabriel Roth, *The Unknowns**
Matthew Yorke, *Chancing It*

ILLUSTRATED
Nicholas Garland, *I wish ...*
Eric McHenry and Nicholas Garland, *Mommy Daddy Evan Sage*
Greg Williamson, *The Hole Story of Kirby the Sneak and Arlo the True*

NON-FICTION
Neil Berry, *Articles of Faith: The Story of British Intellectual Journalism*
Mark Ford, *A Driftwood Altar: Essays and Reviews*
Philip Hoy, ed., *A Bountiful Harvest:*
The Correspondence of Anthony Hecht and William L. MacDonald
Richard Wollheim, *Germs: A Memoir of Childhood*

* Co-published with Picador